1/25,

Tee Patty

the Dancing Preacher

Happy Birthday

Gil Hill

the Dancing Preacher

AN AUTOBIOGRAPHY

"Following God's will for your life is like dancing. You need to allow Him to lead!"

Gil Hill

concierge
PUBLISHING

Omaha, Nebraska

THE DANCING PREACHER

Concierge Publishing books are available from your favorite bookseller or from www.conciergemarketing.com

Concierge Publishing
c/o CMI
13518 L. Street
Omaha, NE 68137

978-1-936840-41-0 (sc)
978-1-936840-42-7 (Mobi)
978-1-936840-43-4 (epub)

Library of Congress Cataloging Number on file with the publisher.

Printed in the USA

10 9 8 7 6 5 4 3

Contents

TO THE READER

For years the voice within has been encouraging me to write a book. When I asked, *What about?* The voice said, "Your life!" When I asked, *Who wants to hear about my life?*, the voice said, "Your family does; your friends do, and I do!" So I asked, *What name shall I give the book?* The voice asked, "What have you been called during your years on planet earth?" I said, *My mom and dad called me "Gilbert;" my sister who couldn't say brother called me "Bub-boo;" in high school I had the nickname "Bub;" in the Navy they called me a seaman and a Yeoman; in college they called me "Gil" and some other names I don't care to mention; as a teacher and athletic coach, they called me "Mr. Hill and Coach;" after seminary, they called me "Reverend and Pastor;" on the cruise ships they called me a dance host; and since moving to Omaha I'm known as "The Dancing Preacher."*

The voice said: "The Bible says, 'The last shall be first,' so the title of the book should probably be *The Dancing Preacher.*" Actually, Nancy, my wife, hears from the same voice, and she also liked the name!

So, here it is, from how I remember the past, and from those who have contributed their input to this book, when asked to help. If there are mistakes, lapses of memory, or if I've missed something or somebody, please forgive me.

This book is dedicated in memory of Melva, the mother of my children, and my wife of 35 years, until God called her home. To Ardyce, my wife for 2 years, and to Nancy, my wife since March 31, 2002.

INTRODUCTION

Although it's a catchy title, I realize that not everyone reading this book can relate to it. Certainly not my children, for I didn't dance much as they were growing up. Definitely not many of the people I served as a minister, for very few of them even knew I could dance.

However, dancing has been instrumental in most of the important things in my life. My mom and dad met at a dance.

My dancing began in high school, continued in the Navy, whenever ashore, and on through my college days.

I met my first wife, Melva, and my current wife, Nancy, at dances. Dancing became less important when I began having a family, traveling, going to seminary, and serving churches.

However, after I retired, dancing came back into my life. It even gave me the opportunity to see the world as a dance host on cruise ships.

Presently, I dance a couple nights a week with my friends at The Ozone, at weddings and on special occasions with Nancy.

Someone asked Nancy why she lets me dance with other women. She politely said, "Because he still thinks he's a dance host, and he always comes home to me!" She could have said, "Because I sing with 'Sweet Adelines' and he dances; I bowl and he plays golf; I cook and he does the dishes." For us, it has worked for thirteen years!

My prayer is that you will enjoy reading my story, and every once in a while find yourself saying, "I didn't know that."

WHO AM I?

I'm a child of God, born into a loving family.

I'm a World War II Veteran.

I'm a sinner saved by God's grace.

I'm a born-again, spirit-filled, Christian believer.

I'm a son, a husband, a father, a grandfather, and a great-grandfather.

I'm an ordained Presbyterian Minister.

I'm a pastor, a teacher, and a counselor.

I'm a dancer and a preacher.

GILBERT: "taken from a cup given to me by my son, David, and family"

Old English: "trusted"

Root: "Gilberto"

Expression: "ability and strength help him achieve his goal"

Personality: "pleasant personality"

Natural: "is a healer, good and wholesome"

Emotional: "someone who believes in being firm, but kind"

Characters: "is full of goodness and love"

Physical: "he attracts others to him"

Mental: "if adversity comes, determination defeats it"

Motivation: "one who creates and invents new things"

Chapter 1

MY BIRTH

All stories have a beginning; mine, of course, was the day I was born. My birth certificate reads: "a boy, born alive, at 4:40pm on April 22, 1926 in the county of Dawes at 111 Morehead Street in Chadron, Nebraska, to Henry Ward B. Hill, age 26, and Dora Ormesher, age 22, and named Gilbert Leslie Hill." It states that one child was stillborn previously. Also, that my dad was born in Jefferson, South Dakota, and was a train baggage man, and my mother was born in Wiggan, England, and was a housewife. The attending physician was M.B. McDowell, who was our family doctor while we lived in Chadron.

Later in life, I learned that my mother's anatomy made child-bearing difficult, and that, after me, two more children either died at birth or shortly thereafter. So, for the birth of my sister, Carolyn, I'm told the decision was made for her to be delivered caesarean, and she was born December 22, 1934, in the hospital in Chadron. I'm sure life would have been different with two brothers and two sisters in the family, but evidently that wasn't to be.

Since they didn't take many baby pictures back then, I've included the first pictures I have from my scrapbook!

Bloomers mom? What did you do to me?

Chapter 2

MY MOM

My mother was born in Wiggan, England, on February 20, 1904 to Frank and Mabel Ormesher and given the name Dora with no middle name. She came to America at age three, and they settled in Chadron, Nebraska, where other members of the Ormesher clan already lived. Subsequently, they became citizens and lived at 106 Mears St, where four girls and two boys were born into the family. My mother's sisters were Edna, Margaret, Edith, Alice, and Gertrude, and the boys were Frank Jr. and Henry. They all attended the same grade school, West Ward, in Chadron, where I also went to grade school. My mother and I even had the same teacher in first grade, Ethel Moorman.

My mother only attended school through the 8th grade, and because she was the oldest child, she became my grandmother's helper in caring for her sisters and brothers. Thus, she was prepared to become the most loving mother a person could ever hope for. However, being of small stature, she had difficulty having children.

My mother was a housewife, but she tried to supplement our limited income by taking in laundry and doing curtains on a stretcher. She never worked outside the home and never learned to drive a car. She was so proud to become a citizen later in life. Her devotion in life was to her family and friends.

She was a member of the Episcopal Church in Chadron and had me christened there with two friends as my godparents. I'm sure my mother took me to church, but I don't have any recollection of going to church as a family. I do remember going to a Baptist Church around age 10 or 11 because a pretty little girl, whose father was the pastor, invited me to visit with her. I liked a game they played in their class called "spin the bottle" because you got to kiss the girl the bottle pointed to.

While living in the house where I was born, my mom told me of the time she left the trap door to the basement open and, in my stroller, I preceded to tumble down the stairs. She came running, shouting, "my baby, my baby!" Guess I survived that fall without any broken bones.

After starting school, I remember coming home on certain days and being told to get my little wagon, walk across the street to the railroad tracks and pick up whatever coal had been spilled in the unloading of the coal cars. Of course, my main concern was that one of my friends might see me doing that and tell others we were poor!

When my dad went off to the Navy in World War II, I became the man of the house at 17. Mother was a great cook and always had delicious meals for Carolyn and me. I didn't like it when she would tell me to go out back and ring a chicken's neck for supper, but that I did many times.

After I came home from the Navy in 1946, I attended college for one year at Chadron State and then loaded my mother and sister into my little VW to travel the 400 miles to Lincoln, where we moved into a converted barracks at Cornhusker Apartments on the former Lincoln Air Base.

From there, we moved to a home on 12th and A in Lincoln, where my folks lived until my dad retired and moved the two of them to a one-bedroom apartment at the Pioneer House. My mother called it the coop; it was mighty small after a two-bedroom house with a full basement.

Mother would leave notes around the apartment for my dad to find reminding him that he had moved them into a chicken coop.

There they lived until she developed dementia and Alzheimer's. She had to go to a nursing home because my sister could not care for her at home any longer. When I was back in town and would visit her, sometimes she would not recognize me. At other times I would ask her if she knew who I was, and she would be respond with, "What a dumb question. You are my son!"

It's very difficult to watch someone you love go through that stage of life. She died on July 12, 1990 at 86 years of age, and I was blessed to conduct her funeral at the Episcopal Church in Lincoln. After cremation, we placed her ashes in a vault in Memorial Park, where my dad's ashes were to be placed beside her upon his death.

I remember how excited she was when I informed her I was going to become a minister. How blessed I am she was my mother, and I will treasure her in my heart until the day I die and meet her in Heaven. I believe Heaven is a better place with her, my dad, and Melva already there!

Chapter 3

MY DAD

My dad was a remarkable man. He was born in Jefferson, South Dakota, on October 2, 1899, and named Henry Ward Brooklyn Hill. He later used the name Ward B. Hill. He was the ninth child born to James Henry Hill and Olive Helen Kellogg with two more children to follow. Two of the girls died in infancy, so my dad grew up with three brothers and five sisters.

The family lived in Jefferson and Burbank, South Dakota, until moving to Chadron, Nebraska. He was in the Army in World War I at age 18. Then, at age 43, he volunteered for the Seabees, which was the construction arm of the Navy during World War II. He returned from serving in the Pacific, to become clerk of the draft board in Chadron. He then accepted a lifetime position with the Veterans Administration in

Lincoln, Nebraska, in 1945. He was a member of the Naval Reserve while living in Lincoln.

After retirement, he and my mother lived in the Pioneer House in Lincoln until he died. As a young man, he homesteaded on a farm out of Harrison, Nebraska, and even taught school near Harrison. When I was born, he was working on the Chicago and Northwestern Railroad. After that, he and his brothers did construction work in and around Chadron. It was the depression years, and finding work was difficult, but they always found a way to pay the bills and feed their families.

The Hill family home in Chadron was at Second and Mears Street. I remember going there, to and from grade school, to see my grandmother. She lived alone in the basement and rented out the upstairs. Her children had grown and moved on, and my grandfather, James, had died in 1916.

Dad's brothers were Wesley, who farmed south of Chadron State Park, Martin, who lived in Alliance and Lloyd, who resided in Sydney. His sisters—Rose, Addie, Lottie, LuVerne, Myrtle, and Grace—were married and lived wherever that took them.

My dad told me how he met my mother at a dance in Chadron. He asked if he could walk her home and at the door said, "When are we going to get married?" After her saying, "I'm not going to marry you," they ended up getting married that same year on June 14, 1923. Dad was 23 and Mother was 19. They had 66 years of wedded bliss, until my mother died at age 86. This story must have stayed in my memory bank because I did almost the same thing when I met Melva some 27 years later!

After mother died, my dad went back to dancing at age 90. On one occasion, when I called him from Kansas, where I was serving a church, he said, "Well, I have a new dance partner!" Then he remarked, "She's a good dancer, and she can drive me home!" He told me he was getting a ride to the dance from the band leader, who had to stay and put things away, which was the reason he needed a ride home.

After I returned to Lincoln in 1991, I was able to spend the last two years of my father's life living near him. I enjoyed taking him out to eat, spending quality time together, and visiting about the past.

His last months were spent first at the Veterans Hospital and later at the same nursing home where my mother had been when she died. On the day he died, I visited him in the morning. When I entered his room, he excitedly asked, "Do you see them?" "See what, dad?" I inquired. "The angels!"

he said. I didn't see the angels, but I believe he did! I wasn't there when he breathed his last breath, but I know the angels came for him, and he is in Heaven with my mother.

My dad died on October 9, 1992 at the age of 93. He was cremated, and his ashes were placed in an urn in the veteran's memorial in Lincoln next to my mother's. I was privileged to officiate at his funeral, and we played dance music for him as we gathered together.

He was truly a very frugal and intelligent man. I'm blessed to have known him as my dad!

Dad and mom in Chadron, circa 1930s

Mom and Dad in Lincoln, circa 1985

Chapter 4

MY SISTER

My sister was born on December 22, 1934 in the hospital in Chadron, Nebraska. Because she was born so close to Christmas, my parents named her Carolyn Joyce: Carol plus Joy!

Since I was nine years old at the time, this little person invaded my private sanctuary. She took up most of my mother's time and attention, which I somehow believed was all mine. Besides that, the relatives doted over her instead of me, and I felt my nose pushed out of place!

As we grew older, because we were so different in age and interests, we didn't really have a lot in common. She and my two girl cousins, Leona and Patti Jo, just didn't seem interested in playing with guns or football with me.

She was only eight when I went off to the Navy, and ten when I started college. Therefore, I was never around much to enjoy her, her friends, or the things she was interested in.

She has worked as a professional photographer and even had her own studio. For as long as I can remember, she has worked as a receptionist at the Lucille Doer Beauty Salon in Lincoln. She recently retired, but still works there part-time.

She married quite young, and now she is a grandmother of nine, and a great-grandmother of 15, loved by all.

I'll always be grateful for the tender, loving care she provided for my dad and mother during their declining health. I was still doing interim ministry in Nebraska, Missouri, and Kansas during most of those years.

We still see each other when we can and talk on the phone from time to time

She is, and always will be, my little sister. I LOVE HER DEARLY!

Carolyn, circa 1950   *Carolyn and me, 1945*

Me and my sister, Carolyn, circa 2012

Chapter 5

GRADE SCHOOL

I walked seven or eight blocks, one way, to attend West Ward Grade School from first through sixth grade. The teachers I remember were Mrs. Moorman, Alma Shipkey and Mrs. Lecher. Back then, grade schools taught the three R's: reading, 'riting, and 'rithmetic, and I liked them all!

I liked my teachers and think they liked me. I was an average student and didn't cause any discipline problems. I'm not sure when it started, but I always liked girls better than boys. Still do; can't dance with boys! I remember kissing a girl for the first time while in the sixth grade. She was mighty pretty, but I can't remember her name!

I had a friend, Wayne Cavender, who I often played with at recess. On one occasion, Wayne tackled me and my left arm separated at the elbow. I left school to go see our doctor, and he put my arm in a sling so natural healing could take place without a cast, but it didn't fully happen as planned. So, I have gone through life with a left arm an inch or so shorter than the right. It hasn't really bothered me in life or as an athlete, however.

In the summer, we had three months off from school, and, at least twice, I spent the summers on my Uncle Wesley's farm south of Chadron. I learned how to milk a cow, stack hay, and do other farm chores. As a city boy, I never took to a bath in a wash tub or using a two- or three-hole outhouse where you used catalog paper instead of toilet paper.

Early in life, I learned how to sell things and was the top salesperson in my class every year for the March of Dimes ten-cent stamps.

One day, while going home from school, I saw two cars collide. I had to go to court as a witness and testify. I don't remember who was at fault, or the outcome, but I liked getting paid for my appearance in court. That was the first and only time I've been in a court room!

6th Grade
Me - 3rd row, 2nd from the right

Chapter 6

JUNIOR AND SENIOR HIGH SCHOOL

When it became time to change schools and enter the seventh grade, we moved to a house on King Street, just three blocks from the Junior-Senior High. At that time, they were both in the same building.

To make spending money, I started selling a weekly paper named *Grit* for five cents. I'd put my money on a buffet in the dining room, until it started disappearing. We discovered the boy delivering our milk was helping himself to the money. My mother devised a way to catch him by hiding in the bedroom and watching through a crack in the door. She caught him in the act, which ended that problem. I also made a little money by meeting the train when the *World-Herald* papers arrived from Omaha, and being first to hit the restaurants and hotels to sell papers.

Our house was on a corner without much grass, so we'd dig little round holes in the ground and play a marble game called pots. The object of the game was to lag marbles from a line a distance away into the hole. The first one in got to keep the marbles for that round. Carolyn reminds me how I taught her to play the game.

From ninth through twelfth grade at Chadron High, athletics and girls became my main interests, and not necessarily in that order. I was popular in school and became president of my class in my junior year. I had the lead in two school plays and was elected co-captain of both the football and basketball team in my senior year. I also ran track and won medals in a number of events.

My team won the Northwest Nebraska Conference Championship in football and lost only one game, which was to Alliance, a Class A school; we were class B. According to the write-up in the local paper, I had a good game against our rival, Crawford, and scored two touchdowns during the game.

We had a so-so record in basketball, but managed to win the Northwest Nebraska tourney, and two of my teammates and I were named to the tournament team. With today's high scores, no one believes me when I say we won that game 20 to 14! Back then, we really played defense.

Academics were another story! Good, but not great. I like to tell people I finished ninth in my class, which is impressive, until I have to fess up that we only had 39 total members.

It was in high school that the girls in my class taught me to dance, along with some older girls missing their boyfriends who were off to war. I liked to go to a ballroom west of town on Saturday nights and dance with all the pretty girls. Betty June E. was my favorite. She now lives in Denver, and we have reconnected many times over the years.

During my junior year, I met Helen Louise, a pretty little blonde with a snubbed nose. She was a senior at Chadron Prep School, and a mutual friend introduced us.

Between my junior and senior year, at age 17, I worked in Alliance, Nebraska on the construction of the Alliance Air Base because the United States was at war with Japan. I drove a truck with a water tank on it and kept the water stations for the workers filled with fresh water. I stayed with a friend in Alliance, and we met some nice girls to dance with in our spare time. What I enjoyed most was my first big paychecks!

During my senior year in high school, I worked on Saturdays at a meat market for my uncle, Ted Ormesher. One day, my mother called to place an order, and Ted told her, "We got some extra meat on display." Fearing the worst, she asked, "What happened?" Ted told her I had sliced off the end of my little finger while cutting some bologna. Fortunately, it didn't require stitches, but I still have the scar!

I didn't realize it at the time, but probably some of the best years of my life were lived in grade school and high school in Chadron.

H.S. Graduation - 1944

Me #47, kneeling in front

Me - back row, 3rd from the right

6 Chadron Boys On Picked Teams

The usual proceedure of selecting the ten best players from conference teams is always a tough job. This year it was more difficult than ever because of the outstanding ability of many players on all teams represented.

Checking and rechecking will prove that many more are deserving of this honor than the ten selected, but there can be no doubt that the boys chosen played their hearts out and are deserving of the highest individual awards. Eleven have been selected instead of ten, providing three centers instead of the usual two.

All Tournament Team

Position	Name	Team
Forward	Geister	Chadron Preps
Forward	Girard	St. Agnes
Forward	Black	Crawford
Forward	Isham	Chadron High
Center	Hill	Chadron High
Center	Essay	St. Agnes
Center	Hawk	Assumption
Guard	T. Brown	Chadron High
Guard	Hartman	Chadron Prep
Guard	Moody	Crawford
Guard	Spath	Gordon

CONFERENCE IS WON BY HI SCHOOL HERE

Cardinals Exhibit Too Much Drive For the Rams

Gilbert Hill leaped into the air among a furious bevy of Crawford Rams, got his glue-fingered hands on the ball, wrestled and twisted until he crossed the goal line for the first six points in an Armistic Day game, which Chadron won 28 to 0.

In the second quarter he again came out of a pass-defending group of opponents with the ball to score again. These two plays were as fine a display of splendid, hard-fighting football as has been seen on any high school gridiron in many years. They were a fine tribute to the spirit of the man that made them, Gilbert Hill, who was celebrating his final game for the Chadron Cardinals.

In the third quarter Bob Isham gauged the middle of the Crawford line three times for six yards a crack; then, when the Rams were all set for the same play, he deftly slipped the ball to guard Tom Brown, who then sped and stiff-armed his way for twenty yards for another score, while the entire baffled Crawford line piled on the clever Isham.

The fourth quarter found the boy with the true and strong right arm, Clayton Brown, rifling another pass to Hill. This time Hill was too well covered, but with a bit of fast headwork, he came up with another gem. Unable to catch the ball, he batted the ball up and beyond the reach of his opponents—alert as a fox, right end Vic Duncan dashed in, caught the ball, eluded one man, shook loose from another and finally fought his way across the line. Later Vic broke through and blocked a punt which rolled out of bounds in the end zone for a safety—two more points. Extra points were made by Rags Thompson and Bowen Bump—whose drop-kick was straight and true and good for fifteen yards more than necessary.

Special mention should also not be forgotten for other fine players of the day. Clayton Brown's spectacular passing which made possible the brilliant catches of Hill. Breath-taking line smashing by Isham, whose best effort was a thrilling off-tackle play which began on the five yard line, and reversing, dodging, stiff-arming, he wasn't tackled until he had covered fifty yards all by himself. Fine punt run-backs by Captain Bill Dierksen, bruising off-tackle thrusts by "Rag" Thompson. Great teamwork on defense led by McNutt, T. Brown and Strom. The greatest thing about these Chadron High Cardinals was their deep seated comradeship and devotion to that fine American tradition—teamwork. This one thing more than any other insured their ending up a very successful season; one defeat in seven games and best of all—the shut-out victory, first time in many seasons, against their traditional fighting foe, Crawford, which to the Chadron boys the undisputed championship of the Northwest Nebraska conference.

After the game the boys were treated to a very delicious chili supper by Mr. and Mrs. McNutt, whose son, Jim, played guard on the team.

Chapter 7

IN THE NAVY!

It was April of 1944, and the U.S. was in the middle of WWII. Germany was on the march across Europe, and Japan had attacked Pearl Harbor. Men were being drafted as soon as they became 18. I would be 18 on April 22nd, with high school graduation still a month or more away. My dad was clerk of the draft board in Chadron and he suggested that I join the Navy because they would let me finish high school.

So, in April, I rode the train to Omaha and joined the Navy. I graduated from high school the last week of May, and on June 3rd, I got back on the train and headed for Farragut, Idaho, where I would go through nine weeks of boot camp. Bob Geister, a friend from Chadron, was on the train with me. When we got there, we were assigned to the same camp, 669, and same barracks. After getting shots for every disease you can think of, we laid down in our bunks, both arms dangling down the side, until we could get some rest and face the next day.

While there, I organized a track team, including Bob, two friends, and myself. We competed in the mile relay against other camps and came away with a victory. I also entered a cross country race and helped my camp win first place. We were awarded a coveted one day liberty to a nearby town. The only girls I got to see in my nine weeks at boot camp were on that day! There was no time for dancing though!

After finishing boot camp, we were given one week's leave back home before reporting for a duty assignment. While home, I bought an engagement ring, which cost a huge $20 and gave it to Helen Louise. Then it was back to Farragut, and a trip by rail to San Francisco, for duty as a seaman second class. I was assigned to the *U.S. Manderson Victory*, a converted merchant marine ship, scheduled to carry ammunition to the battleships, cruisers, and destroyers in the Pacific.

Helen Louise's sister lived in Oakland, California and she came out to see me before I was to sail away. We thought about getting married in California, but a chaplain talked me out of it, saying, "You are only 18, and you are off to war. If you return, and your engagement is still on, you can always get married then!" It was great advice! I never did marry the girl. We went our separate ways while I was on duty, but remained friends!

After boarding the ship, I learned we had a complement of only fifty sailors and five officers. You soon got to know everyone! The first thing we did was a "shakedown cruise," from San Francisco to Los Angeles and back, to prove the ship seaworthy. Then we began loading almost 8,000 tons of ammunition from the Ordinance Depot in Frisco.

In December 1944, we sailed out under the Golden Gate Bridge, into the Pacific Ocean, and on to Pearl Harbor. As we entered Pearl, we were able to view some of the terrible destruction the Japanese had caused in their 1941 attack—a scene I'll never forget!

From there, our orders took us past the Islands, where war had taken place, and alongside ships of our fleet needing ammo. Finally, we ended up in Leyte Gulf in the Philippines, and, from there, to the invasion of Okinawa. There were so many ships in the bay off Okinawa; you couldn't count them, and the kamikazes could be seen diving at them. Thank God, they didn't come close to us, or it would have blown up the entire harbor. After that battle ended, we were ordered back to Leyte Gulf.

One day, in the many months we were at sea, an announcement came over the loudspeaker, stating that the ship's office needed someone who could use a typewriter, which I had learned in school. I hustled to the office and applied, even though I'd been told you should never volunteer for anything in the Navy. I became an assistant to the ship's clerk; the Navy term for that is Yeoman. An office, a promotion to Yeoman third class, and a pay raise came with the job. Later on, I became a Yeoman second class, with another pay raise.

In August 1945, we received word that the U.S. had dropped two atomic bombs on Japan. The Japanese surrendered, and the war was over! Beer flowed freely that day! The war was over, and we would be going home!

We remained in Leyte Gulf, with nothing to do, for three months, awaiting orders. Finally, we sailed for the states, and ended up in Port Angeles, Washington. It was just in time to go home on leave for Christmas and be with family and friends again.

The weekends in and around Seattle were fun. I found some young ladies to dance with, and spent some time with one of my cousins, Helen Hill. One day, while walking down a street in Seattle, I bumped into one of my high school teachers who had moved to a teaching job in Seattle. What a small world!

In January of 1946, we finally received orders to go to New York for decommissioning of the ship. I never understood why we couldn't do that where we were, but I found out the government never does things the easy way, so we sailed down the west coast, through the Panama Canal to Puerto Rico, encountering a storm that almost sank the ship with enormous waves, lightning all around, and torrents of rain. This was the type of storm where not a soul would be on deck because they were too afraid of being washed overboard – we were all hunkered down in quarters wide awake.

We finally made it to Puerto Rico, where we picked up a load of sugar to take to New York. After arriving in New York, we sat in the Naval Yard for a couple months while awaiting further individual orders. I had a number of weekends in New York and found a "dime a dance" place, where I met some pretty girls that were willing to dance with me.

Finally, I received orders saying I could go home for a couple weeks to see family and friends, and then report to Great Lakes Naval Station for discharge.

My discharge came on June 20, 1946, two years and seventeen days after joining the Navy. I'd gone on the ship a Seaman second class and, in my time aboard, had advanced to Yeoman second class, a move of three pay grades. I considered signing up for another four years and making the Navy a career, but my desire for the home front prevailed, so it was back to Chadron and civilian life.

Age 18

Age 20

Chapter 8

BACK HOME

With my Navy days over, I went back home to Chadron. I'd sent over $600 home while overseas, and with it, I bought my first car, a 1936 dark green Willys. My dad had already moved to Lincoln to start a new job, so Mom, Carolyn, and I stayed in Chadron until we finished the school year and lived at 106 Mears Street. Grandma Mabel was living next door in the new house Grandpa Frank had built before he died.

Helen Louise had moved to Omaha, and I heard she married a man named Mountain. My friends used to kid me and say, "She traded up from a Hill to a Mountain!"

In September, I enrolled in college at Chadron State and went out for football. I made the team, but badly sprained an ankle in the first game, ending my season. After joining a town basketball team, I took three friends in my car to play in a game in Edgemont, South Dakota. On the way there, I missed a turn on a gravel road and turned the car over, rolling twice into a ditch. Because the running boards had folded up against the doors, no one was ejected; all we had were bumps and bruises. Another car came along and took us to the game.

I can't remember if we won or lost, because my mind was focusing on the fact that we had to catch a ride home. Another player agreed to take us home, and when the car I was in pulled up in front of our house, my mother met me at the door, crying and saying, "I know something bad has happened." Mother's intuition!

A few days later, I had a friend help me tow the car back to town, and I made the decision to repair it. It took almost three months until I had wheels again. I had to either walk or bum a ride to college, movies, and dances. It was no fun!

I began dating a girl who was a professor's aide at college, which led to straight A's in that class! When the Willys was running again, my friends and I liked to drive to neighboring towns for dances. My government check paid for most of the school bills, and I worked at the Red Owl Grocery Store to make enough money to buy clothes and cover other expenses. Although I never had much money, I always seemed to have enough!

I celebrated my 21st birthday on April 22, 1947 at Joe's Bar, our favorite, in Chadron with friends, drinking boilermakers, which is a stein of beer with a shot of whiskey in the middle. I can't say that I remember much about that night, which means I probably had a great time!

In the summer of 1947, Dad wanted us to move to Lincoln, so we loaded up my little car, and the three of us headed out with just the clothes on our backs and a few suitcases. It was a 400 mile trip, and it took us two days. My dad had rented a small two-bedroom apartment in Huskerville, which was a small community that had developed in a converted barracks at the old Air Force base, just north of Lincoln.

We hadn't lived there long when a young widow with two little boys moved in next door. I found out that she liked to dance, so we hit Kings Ballroom on a regular basis. Her brother-in-law convinced her that she needed an older man with a job and stability to help raise her two boys, rather than a college jock, so we parted company as friends. We moved to Lincoln, and she moved back in with her mother. I heard she married a man named Marymee and they lived happily ever after!

My first suit and fancy shoes, age 21

The wrecked car, a Willys, 1936

Chapter 9

COLLEGE IN LINCOLN

In August of 1947, Dad bought a house at 12th & A Street in Lincoln, and we moved from Huskerville. I enrolled at the University of Nebraska for my second year of college and transferred 30 credit hours from Chadron. I didn't like NU from the get-go. There were too many students in each class; I didn't know anyone, and I didn't relate to the professors. I spent a lot of time at a downtown pool hall, where I met Bruce Neiman, who became my best friend. He helped me on many of my subsequent moves from city to city and state to state.

At mid-semester, I transferred to Nebraska Wesleyan University in University Place in Lincoln. By that time, the Willys had seen its last legs, and I traded up to a 1938 Chevy. Back and forth from home to college was a 30 minute trip, one way, and I was looking for a way to cut the driving time down. That's when Paul Brettman, who became another lifetime friend, invited me to join the Crescent Fraternity and move into their frat house.

Of course, I still went home with my laundry on most weekends, but I spent the remainder of my college days living in the frat house. I even became house manager the last two years, which meant free rent. The members of the fraternity were mostly athletes, and some girls gave us the reputation of being "the boozers!" We were just guys who liked to have fun, and if that meant having a few beers and dancing, then so be it! The Crescent Fraternity is where I made friendships that were life changing and long lasting. Primarily, Bob Ketterer, Cliff Squires, Aldie Johnson, Jim Porter, Rollie Wiegers, Harris Hollie, Paul Brettman and Herb Rihn, who became my roommate.

I began attending classes with a goal of becoming a high school athletic coach and teacher. Bus Knight, the football and track coach at the time, invited me to come out for track, so I did. I ended up on the mile relay team with Cal Bones, Jack Cudabach, and Aldie Johnson. We ended up winning gold medals in a number of track meets. I also ran the 220 and 440, which back then were yards, not meters. I became a member of the "W," or Wesleyan club and lettered three years in track. Coach suggested I go out for football if I intended to coach, so I went out for football my senior year and lettered in that sport also.

Since I was now a college jock, Irv Peterson, the basketball coach, asked me to be his student trainer. That's where I learned how to tape ankles, give massages, and take care of a team's physical needs. This experience served me well later in life as a coach.

Our sister sorority was the Willards, and at dances with them, my expertise as a dancer served me well. I never lacked for a young, beautiful girl wanting to learn how to dance. The Crescents had an annual Bowery Party, and often a Crescent and Willard were found pairing up at the party. I liked to take a girl I'd met at Kings Ballroom named Dorothy L., who had been elected Miss Lincoln in 1948, to the dances with me. I dated a number of other girls, but Dorothy was my go-to-girl while I was at Wesleyan. Of course, the college girls weren't too pleased with my bringing in a "street girl!"

Three years at NWU produced the kind of memories that will last forever. Even today, I still have four college classmates on my emails. I'll always treasure those days; they set the stage

for one of the biggest chapters in my life—1950!
Fasten your seat-belt; let's meet Melva!

1950s – Big Changes in Everyone's Life

Everything changed in the 1950s. Television changed the way we lived. The Russians and Sputnik were on our minds. When the Russians sent Laika into space suddenly, we needed to raise our kids to be better scientists and mathematicians.

Ed Sullivan brought Elvis and the Beatles right into our living rooms.

The New York Yankees were on screens across the United States, with Casey Stengel at the helm, leading stars such as Whitey Ford, Mickey Mantle, and Yogi Berra smiling and waving as if we were there with them.

Highways were built, making transportation easier all across the states. As a result, people traveled more, Holiday Inns were popping up for travelers along these routes.

Shopping centers brought everything into one place for easy access in every neighborhood in every corner of the country, so people could begin their habit of buying things they don't need in quantities too large for their families. This was good for the burgeoning economy.

At the same time, the Civil Rights Movement was born when Rosa Parks made history by refusing to leave her seat on the bus.

The United States of America grew from 48 states to 50.

And so it went...

Crescent Fraternity - 1950
Me - 2nd row - 2nd from the right

1949

College, age 24, 1950

Chapter 10

MEETING AND MARRYING MELVA

I n May of 1950, I graduated college and signed a contract to coach and teach at the high school in Table Rock, Nebraska in the fall.

The first week in June, Bruce and I decided to drive to Crete, Nebraska, on Saturday night, and check out the dance at Tuxedo Park. There I saw a beautiful girl with dark hair, and asked her to dance. She said, "No, thanks. I don't know you!" Bill B., a friend from Doane College that I'd ran against in track, saw what happened, came over, and asked me if I'd like to meet the girl. I said, "Of course." He introduced me to Melva Clough. Once again, I asked her to dance, and this time she said, "Yes."

I found out she was from Beatrice, Nebraska, and was there with some girlfriends. We danced a number of times that night, and I asked if I could have her phone number. She gave it to me and after the dance was over, we went our separate ways.

I thought about her a lot in the week to follow and finally called to see if I could drive to Beatrice on Saturday night and take her dancing. She agreed, and it became our first date. At the time, I was working as caddy master at the Lincoln Country Club, so didn't get off until six p.m. But after a shower and change of clothes, I headed for Beatrice, 40 miles from Lincoln, and then we drove another 30 miles to a dance in Maryville, Kansas.

After that, dating became a weekend event through June and July. I didn't know until much later, but Melva told her sister she'd met the man she was going to marry. On the first weekend in August, I gave her my fraternity pin as an engagement ring, and asked her to marry me. She said, "Yes." We were married on August 20 in the Methodist Church in Beatrice by Dr. Alvie Clark. I was 24, and she was 20, and it was a marriage made in Heaven. We didn't even listen to those that said, "Wow, after only 10 weeks of knowing each other, isn't it too soon?"

Thirty-five years later, with three children and four grandchildren, we both knew God had brought us together and blessed our union.

Melva's sister, Rosie Bridgewater, was her matron of honor, and Herb Rihn was my best man. Barb Roland was one of her bridesmaids, and Bob Ketterer was one of my groomsmen. After meeting at our wedding, Bob and Barb ended up getting hitched a couple years later. Some of my fraternity brothers came through the reception line with a handshake and something I had to stuff in my pocket which is used to prevent pregnancy! I'm not sure I ever used any of them!

Melva was working at the time for Dr. Herb Jackson as a dental assistant. We considered her living at home, continuing to work to save money, and my driving back and forth to Table Rock, but we decided we'd rather begin marriage living together, even if we didn't have any money. My teaching job was to pay a huge $300 a month, and we thought we could make it. Young love will do that!

The wedding was on a Sunday, and I was scheduled to begin football practice the next day, so after the reception was over, we drove some thirty miles to spend the night in our one bedroom apartment above a Beauty Salon. The ducks quacking out back provided all-night music for our honeymoon suite.

Thus began my life as a married man and as a high-school coach and teacher. Still with me? It gets better!

Wedding Picture, August 20, 1950

Chapter 11

LIFE IN TABLE ROCK

On Monday, August 21, we began football practice. We were a class D school, still playing 11-man football. The first day of practice, I counted 18 would-be players. When I asked where the others were, one lad said, "This is it, coach!" Whenever I needed to have a scrimmage, I had to invite some former grads and join them just to have enough players.

On the first day at school, I saw this tall boy walking down the hall. I asked him, "What is your name, and why aren't you out for football?" He told me he was Junior Karas, and his mother wouldn't let him play because he needed to wear glasses, and they cost too much. The next day, I paid his mother a visit, and told her I would furnish unbreakable glasses and a face mask if she'd let him play. I think I also gave her the Gil Hill charm because she agreed to let him play.

Junior scored the first touchdown in our first game of the season, which we won. He played center on the basketball team, and was our leading scorer. At the state track meet, he scored 20 points, placing first in the broad jump, a tie for first in the high jump, and first in the low hurdles. Someone else scored five points, and we came within two points of winning state. Without a doubt, Junior was one of the best athletes I ever had the chance to coach.

Melva and I stayed in Table Rock for two years. I taught business subjects and coached three sports: football, basketball and track. Sometimes I'd get a little vociferous on the bench or sidelines; that's stating it mildly! I remember a time where I got on the referee at a basketball game who happened to be my classmate, Cliff Squires, from Wesleyan. I was constantly yelling, "Bad call!" or "You missed that one!" He came over and said, "Sit down and shut up, Gil, or I'll have to call a technical on you!" I didn't argue with Cliff; he was bigger than me, and he had the whistle.

The school colors were orange and black, and the mascot was a tiger, so for our annual school yearbook, I submitted the name "TIG-OR-ACK," and it was accepted as the cover for 1951.

I'd stayed in the Naval Reserve to make extra money by attending monthly meetings, and when the Korean Conflict broke out, I was recalled by the Navy. I went to Omaha for a physical, and, lo and behold, the doctor was from Beatrice and knew Melva. I told him we were recently married, and I had a bad back from a football injury. After giving me a complete physical exam, he gave me a medical discharge. That ended my naval career!

Melva got a job at the local restaurant waiting tables, and, because money was tight, we gave up one room, the bedroom, of our three room apartment, and we slept on a hide-a-bed in the living room. She attended all our home games, some out-of-town games, and supported me in whatever I did. She even got me to go to the Methodist Church with her on Sundays! I doubt I heard much of what the lady preacher had to say, but some gospel seeds were planted that bore fruit later in life. I don't know if it was the cold winter or the hard bed, but we found out in March of 1952 that Melva was pregnant with our first child.

It was about then that my friend from college, Bob Ketterer, called and wanted to know if I'd like to come to Blair, Nebraska, and coach athletics with him. I accepted the offer and we made plans to move during the summer.

Life was good in Table Rock and valuable lessons were learned about working with teenagers and their parents, and about being a teacher and coach. I've stayed in touch with members of the teams and the classes of 1951 and 1952. The '52 class still invites me to their class reunions, and I've gone a number of times. I never expected to outlive some of those I taught and coached, but that too has happened.

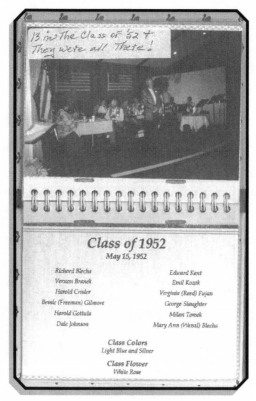

60th Reunion - 2012

Chapter 12

LIFE IN BLAIR

We left Table Rock shortly after school was out in 1952, spent a couple months in Lincoln with my parents, and then went on to get settled in the Blair Apartments before football practice was to start in August. I soon met Earl Pace, who became an assistant coach, along with me, and Bob was the head coach. In basketball, Bob had the A team and I had the B team. We each had our duties in track, and I coached baseball with Earl's help. My classroom teaching consisted of business subjects, with an emphasis on bookkeeping.

Melva was a stay-at-home mom while expecting our first child. She was glad to be reunited with her high school friend, Barb Rowland, and spent quality time with her while in Blair. Bob and Barb were newlyweds at that point.

It soon came time for Melva to give birth. Melva was to be 22 on October 1st, and it looked like the baby might be born on her birthday because she was experiencing pains. The Blair hospital was nothing more than a converted rooming house, but it was clean and close to the house. The proximity came in handy that day as we rushed to the hospital for what turned out to be false labor. After a few hours at the hospital, waiting on pins and needles, the doctor came out and said, "You can take your wife home and come back tomorrow!" No baby today!

We went back to the hospital on October 2nd. When the doctor finally came out, he announced that I was the proud father of a healthy, beautiful, blonde baby girl, born at 11:30 p.m. We later named her Pamela Sue.

I'd made a number of friendly wagers that my first child would be a boy, so had to pay up when a beautiful blonde girl joined us. What a blessing she has been through our years together. She has always been my pride and my joy! It's hard to believe that she is now a mother of two boys and a girl, and a grandmother of nine! She has her mother's sweet disposition and charm, and my smile and facial features. Her husband, Gary, says she looks more like me every day.

I don't recall the exact date, but Bob and I were with the basketball team in a town north of Blair, and after the game we stopped in a local bar to peek at a cold one! We met a man there who worked as a salesman for National Cash Register. After getting acquainted, he said they were looking for a salesman to work out of Lincoln, and asked if I'd be interested in checking out the job. To make a long story short, I did, and accepted their offer. We left Blair in June of '54, and moved to an apartment just three blocks from my folks in Lincoln.

The job paid well for a trainee, but it wasn't my cup-of-tea! They put me, a people person, down in the basement of their store in Lincoln to learn how cash registers worked before I could go out and sell anything! It didn't take long for me to realize I'd made a mistake, so I decided to check in with the teaching agency, Davis, that had placed me in Table Rock, and see what was out there.

We spent two great years in Blair and made friends I still see now and then. Mainly Hugh Hunt and Bob Madsen and their wives; but also the members of the class of '54, who have invited me to many of their class reunions to deliver talks for inspiration and a few jokes. At their 60th reunion in 2014, Jane Hunt greeted me after dinner with these nice words, "Gil, you are more alive spiritually, mentally, and physically than most of us!"

Another move coming up! Stay with us as we go to Pueblo, Colorado!

Me and Pam - 1953

Bob Madsen, Me, Hugh Hunt
60 Years later, 2013, at our high school reunion

Chapter 13

LIFE IN PUEBLO, COLORADO

In the fall of 1955 I received a call from the Davis Teacher's Employment Agency in Lincoln. They informed me that the superintendent of schools from Pueblo, Colorado, was coming to town looking for teachers, and asked if I would be interested in an interview.

After my meeting with him and talking it over with Melva, we agreed to move to Pueblo to teach high school Social Studies beginning mid-term.

So, right after Christmas, we loaded up our meager belongings and moved to a little one-bedroom apartment in Pueblo. I didn't realize it at the time, but this was probably the biggest move of my life, for it was in Pueblo that I met Jesus Christ as my personal savior! However, I'm getting ahead of all the wonderful things that happened in that steel city on the Arkansas River!

Melva and I bought our first house there. David, our first son, was born there on June 5, 1956, and our second son, Dennis, was born there on October 10, 1957. Also, I began a new and interesting career as a "fundraiser" for start-up companies.

One day, in the teacher's lounge, a friend told me about a new company being formed in Colorado called the Colorado Corporation, and asked if I would be interested in helping them sell stock. I'd recently moved from the classroom to being a Distributive Education instructor at both high schools, which gave me access to a lot of people in business, so I jumped at that opportunity on a part-time basis. That stock issue soon sold out. One of the salesman I'd met, Joe Cannady, came down from Denver, and asked me to join him and others in selling stock in State Life of Colorado. While we were doing that, he introduced me to a Southern Baptist preacher, Ed Ashley.

Ed was very persistent in inviting us to attend church. We finally accepted and traveled clear across town almost every Sunday to attend Belmont Baptist Church. There I heard the gospel message in a way that convicted me of sin, and convinced me of the need for salvation. The Holy Spirit eventually pushed me down the aisle to give my life to the Lord. Later on, Melva and I made our professions of faith, were baptized by immersion, and joined the church. Little did I realize where that would ultimately lead!

Back to the boys! A few months after David was born, the doctor told us his eyes had been damaged by the instruments in the birth process, and he needed to wear corrective glasses. Imagine expecting a 6 month boy to leave his glasses on! As new Christians, we prayed God would provide a better answer. We were led to a doctor who, on the first visit said, "I believe I can correct the problem with surgery!" The surgery was completed, and we learned about miracles. As the doctor came out of surgery, he said, "The operation came out in a way I always hope for, but seldom expect, and I was able to correct your boy's eyes."

The next miracle came with Dennis. While in the hospital for a case of bronchitis, he came down with a germ that was killing babies in hospitals nationwide called staphylococcus! One night, while out making calls, I stopped by the hospital to find Dennis in an oxygen tent. As the doctor came into his room, he said, "We've done all we can; it's out of my hands!" After the doctor left, I dropped to my knees in that room, and prayed to God. *Dear Lord, if You will save this boy's life, I will give You mine.* I learned it's not wise to put God to the test, for within a week the doctor called and said, "I've got good news—your boy is getting better." God performed His miracle, and I kept my vow, although it took another three years for me to realize just where that vow would lead.

While selling stock in State Life, I met Bill Freda, in Canyon, Colorado. He helped me sell some stock there and called one day to say he had two friends who'd like to meet me. They wanted someone to sell a stock issue to build a tourist attraction called Buckskin Joe near the Royal Gorge. I took on the job, and, with the help of Bill and a friend, we sold out the issue in a few months.

Unfortunately, the venture wasn't a money maker. Years later I learned it was bought out of bankruptcy by the Royal Gorge Corporation, owned by the Murchisons of Texas oil fame. I still have some worthless share certificates in a file drawer.

Another move coming up!

(Back) Me holding Dennis, Melva
(Front) Pam and David

Chapter 14

LIFE IN BROOMFIELD, COLORADO

In 1960, a business friend called and asked me to move to Denver and become part of a new investment firm he and some others had started. I accepted his offer and moved to Broomfield, Colorado—a new housing development north of Denver. Dick Bridgewater, my brother-in-law, and his brother, Dale, were in the real estate business there, and found us a nice three bedroom, full basement house.

Across the street from us was a farmhouse where the owner agreed to keep a horse I'd acquired in a stock trade. That horse just didn't like Pam, who was eight years old at the time. Every time I'd try to put her on the horse, it would start bucking. Needless to say, she never rode the horse.

Doctor Gordon lived in the house north of us and became our family doctor. When David was four, he fell through a window well and cut his leg badly. Doctor Gordon sewed it up, but he still has the scar to prove it.

Dennis, who was three, was full of mischief as always, and one day decided to paint the neighbor's car with a brush left in a can of turpentine by the owner. Fortunately, the paint was so thin we were able to clean the mess off the car. Whenever we'd try to discipline that boy, he'd just look up at us and laugh.

We found a newly-formed Baptist Church and joined up. Before long, I was teaching a class, asked to become a deacon, and did some supply preaching. When it became time to call a pastor, I became chairman of the pulpit committee. Finally, we called E.K. Shepherd from Muleshoe, Texas, who was the answer to our prayers. E.K. was both my pastor and my advisor in preparing me for life as a minister.

Pam was in school, the boys were growing up, and Melva was a stay-at-home mom. I was running around the country in a cherry red, '56 Caddy, making more money than I ever had. Life was good, and we thought we were in Broomfield to stay. We soon found out that God had other plans for us. Another chapter in our lives was about to begin.

Chapter 15

LIFE AS A TRAVELING MAN!

Early in 1961, Joe Cannady called and asked me to fly to Rapid City, South Dakota, in his private plane and consider taking over the selling of a stock issue in the South Dakota Corporation. He'd been doing that for six months and his wife wanted him to give it up and stay home.

After checking it out, I rented a house in Rapid City and began commuting by air from Denver to Rapid City. I traveled around South Dakota holding sales meetings and encouraging the twenty salesmen. My golf clubs were always in the trunk, and I often found time to visit a golf course after a day's work. Melva and the children came to live with me during the summer months. We enjoyed sight-seeing at Mount Rushmore and Dinosaur Park.

After completing that stock issue, we returned to Broomfield in time for the children to start school. Then a man in Sioux Falls, South Dakota, called and asked me to help sell a stock issue in a new company. I decided to do that until the end of the year and commuted by air between Denver and Sioux Falls.

I remember driving down a highway north of Sioux Falls one day, when one of the many pheasants they are noted for flew out of a ditch. Before I could maneuver out of the way, the bird hit my windshield on the driver's side at a high rate of speed. I had a shattered windshield and a dead bird in my lap. Soon after I pulled off the road, a friendly state trooper happened by and helped put a cover over the windshield. I was still able to drive the car, so he led me slowly into the next town. I was forced to rent a car until mine could be repaired.

All the running around the country, only being home now and then, was taking its toll on me and my family. Plus, all this time, my prayers were being interrupted by a still, small voice saying, "I have something bigger and better for you to do!"

While having a meal at their home, Bonnie Ashley, wife of the pastor who led me to the Lord said, "Gil, you need to stop running and go into Christian ministry!" On another occasion, a person I met said, "You sound like a preacher!"

My pastor in Broomfield had accepted a call to a church in Texas, and the church asked me to give the sermon whenever I was in town.

Early in 1962, after much prayer and seeking the Lord, Melva and I decided we would pursue a life in the ministry, wherever that would lead. Later, she liked to tell her relatives and friends, "I prayed for years that Gil would become a Christian, but I never once prayed he would become a minister!"

We told Ed Ashley about our decision, and he gave my name to a Baptist Church in La Vita, Colorado, in need of a Sunday preacher. That led to my driving 200 miles round trip every weekend, weather permitting, to share the gospel with the 15 to 20 people who might attend church that Sunday. Since I didn't know how to prepare a sermon, I just started sharing my testimony. Sometimes the family would go with me and we'd make a weekend of it. We would spend the night in the home of one of the church members and be treated to a hearty breakfast. We met some loving, caring people in that little church. God was at work in preparing me for life to follow.

I remember the first time I preached in La Vita. As I was leaving, their pulpit supply person gave me $35, a dozen eggs, and the frozen meat of a cut-up rabbit. I'd already been told this about the ministry, "The hours are long, and the pay is meager, but you can't beat the retirement plan!"

Thus began a new venture in faith!

Chapter 16

PREPARING FOR MINISTRY

Having made the decision to prepare for gospel ministry, we spent the first months of 1962 getting things in order to move. First, however, we had to decide where to go to seminary. The choices were Golden Gate in California or Midwestern in Kansas City. I believe our Nebraska roots helped sway us toward Kansas City, and thus we proceeded in faith that God would lead the way.

We announced our decision toward gospel ministry to our family and friends. That spring, I received a call from an insurance man in Lincoln, Nebraska, offering me a job with a sizeable salary to come to Lincoln, and help sell stock in a new company he was putting together. I told the man I'd already made a decision to take on a bigger job!

I still had to make a living to put food on the table, so I started selling a combination of life insurance and mutual fund products. I did so well that the insurance company had us come to the home office in Amarillo, Texas. As their leading salesman in a contest, they presented Melva with her first and only fur coat. Pam still has it!

I sold the Cadillac, which left us with only a Plymouth Station Wagon and I began to convert all stocks and bonds to cash. I decided to sell the house myself to avoid real estate commission. Thus began another experience in trusting the Lord. We made plans to move the second week in August, in order to begin school in September. Guess when the house finally sold? The first week in August! I was learning to trust God, who does all things well!

We said our goodbyes to our family and friends in Broomfield and loaded a moving van with furniture. The van was to meet us in Kansas City sometime after August 15th. We figured that would give us ample time to travel, find a place to live, and enroll in the seminary before the furniture arrived. Wouldn't you know it, I walked into the seminary office on August 14th, and the receptionist says, "Good thing you are here, Mr. Hill; we just received a call saying your furniture will be here in a few hours."

Fortunately, they knew of a vacancy in Liberty, Missouri, 30 miles from Kansas City, so we made arrangements to unload there. We were in the process of unloading the van at that location, when the seminary office called. They had a home for rent just a couple miles north of the seminary, so back on the van went the furniture. We spent the night in a motel and finally got settled in the next day.

Soon the move began to take shape. I registered for classes at the seminary; we made school arrangements for Pam and David, and got acquainted with the neighbors and the stores for shopping.

On the first day of school, six year old David cried, and didn't want to get on the bus. Who could blame him? Leaving home for the first time, going off with total strangers, plus the trauma of another move. I hate to admit it, but I was as scared as he was about the changes we were making.

UP NEXT—LIFE AT THE SEMINARY!

Chapter 17

SEMINARY LIFE

I was 36 years old, and it was September 1962, when I embarked on a 3 year study toward a degree of Bachelor in Ministry. Pam and David were in school, Melva was staying home with Dennis, and a lot of adjustments were being made in our lives.

I was taking courses in Hebrew, Greek, Homiletics, which is learning how to preach, church history and many more. In my first semester of Hebrew, my teacher, Dr. Roy Honeycutt, asked me to be his grader, so I would go home from school and grade papers until the kids came home, and then it was supper time. Melva accepted a job at the seminary working the switchboard and greeting those who were visiting the seminary.

We began to make new friends in the seminary family and at the church we attended. Two of my best friends were David Hood and "Dude" Woodson, whose real name is Layoid. Melva and I adopted Dude and his wife; we had them over for meals, and helped them through a difficult time in their marriage. David Hood has passed on to glory, but Dude and I still keep in touch by email. He went on to get his doctorate and is the pastor of a church in Oklahoma.

A young black man from Kenya enrolled as a student, and I was in charge of helping him get acquainted. I learned his name, Daniel Mbye, where the "M" stands for the fact he was born in April. Since he didn't know the exact date, I gave him mine, April 22, so we could celebrate our birthday together. We often had him over for a meal. On one occasion, he brought his new girlfriend, who was also black. After they left, Pam, who was now eleven, says, "I like Daniel's girlfriend, and, besides that, they match!" Daniel returned to Kenya to teach and preach, and, unfortunately, I lost track of him.

My second year at the seminary, I ran for student body president and was elected. Probably because I was older than most of the other students, or maybe because I was the only candidate. One of my duties was to introduce the chapel speakers.

On one occasion, the speaker was James Jeffrey, Director of The Fellowship of Christian Athletes. Over a cup of coffee, after his chapel talk, we found we had common experiences in athletics, and he asked me to get involved in FCA. I joined then, and I'm still an active member. I've had FCA speakers at the churches I was pastor of, started an FCA group in Clovis while there, and served on the state board of FCA after returning to Nebraska.

The second summer at seminary, the house we'd been renting was sold. After looking around, we rented a house with a swimming pool where I could make a little extra money. I gave beginner's swimming lessons to a group of kids under twelve. Some of these kids made the experience a blast.

Another time, I announced to the boys' class that we were going to get in the deep end of the pool that day, which was five feet. One little guy informed me that he wasn't going to go in. When I asked, "Why not?" he said, "Cause I'm chicken!" Another time, a boy came up missing, so, as soon as the class was over, I called his home. His mother informed me that he'd walked home. That was a big time relief!

While in seminary, many of us would drive a school bus to help pay expenses. It was a tough job, trying to keep a load of junior high kids quiet! One lad was causing a big disturbance and wouldn't sit down, so I stopped the bus, got him by the collar, and put him out by the side of the road. That got his attention! He thought I was really going to leave him there. I never had any problem with that lad again!

We were always looking for a place to preach, and the seminary kept a list of churches who needed Sunday pulpit supply, so our family traveled almost every Sunday to a country or a small town church to preach the gospel. Usually, a church family would take us home with them for dinner. I don't remember the town, but, on one occasion, we were sitting around the table with a family on a Sunday, and the lady of the house asked me to have the blessing, so I did. The meal was fried chicken, mashed potatoes, and green beans or corn, with dessert to follow. We had finished the main course and were waiting for the dishes to be cleared before the dessert. After it was placed on the table, we were waiting for everyone to be seated again. A youngster rolled his eyes, looked at me, and said, "Do you all pray before the dessert too?"

Unexpected blessings and more to come! Hollywood coming up!

Chapter 18

HOLLYWOOD

No, I'm not talking about Hollywood in California. Actually, I considered going there when someone told me I looked like Joseph Cotton, the film star. I decided I'd rather be one of God's stars, so I'm talking about serving a church in Kansas City, Missouri.

In my final year at seminary, one of my classmates told me he preached at a church in Kansas City, and couldn't go back because he had another job. He asked if I'd like to go there on Sunday. Since I had no other place to go, he gave me the name and phone number of the person to contact. As we were parting, he said, "Oh, by the way, it's a Presbyterian church."

I was Christened as an infant in the Episcopal Church, attended a Methodist College, married in the Methodist Church, saved and baptized in the Baptist Church, attending a Baptist seminary, and was now being asked to preach at a Presbyterian Church. The church denomination didn't matter to me.

Sunday we loaded up the station wagon and headed over to 43rd and Jackson in Kansas City to Hollywood Presbyterian Church, where we were met by George Barth. They'd prepared a pot-luck dinner, and, after dinner, George asked if I could come back the following Sunday. Of course, I said yes, which led to a month of Sundays. Then George said, "We like you and your family, and we have an empty manse. [Baptists call them parsonages] Would you consider moving in and being our supply preacher until you finish seminary?" Little did he know, our bank account was down to a few dollars, and we didn't know how we were going to pay the next month's rent. Of course, the God we serve was supplying our need in a way we hadn't anticipated.

To make a long story longer, we moved during Christmas vacation to 4224 Spruce Street, just two blocks from the church, intending to stay until graduation from seminary. Two years later, we were still there! Valuable lessons were being learned about race relations in a way we'd never experienced before. Pam was in the sixth grade, David the second, and Dennis the first.

This was an area of town which had been torn up by a new interstate highway and was in rapid transition. White people were moving to the suburbs, and black people were moving into the area. Pam and one other girl were the only white girls in their class. David and Dennis had only a few white kids in theirs. At school, they began to encounter reverse racial prejudice. Black girls would make fun of Pam and the way she dressed. Black boys would pick fights with our boys, and one stole a baseball glove from Dennis. Melva and Pam taught Sunday school, and a few black kids came, but no parents. The average attendance in church services was 25 people. Mostly those wanting to keep the church doors open. God had me right where He wanted me. I learned how to minister to their needs.

In the Spring of 1965, I graduated from seminary with a Bachelor of Ministry degree. My mom and dad came down from Lincoln for the graduation services. Life was good, and I was ready for whatever God had in store.

The Kansas City Chiefs were new in town and someone gave us tickets to some of their games. At one of them, Dennis got separated from us in the crowd. I thought he was with Pam, and she thought he was with me. I called Melva, hoping he'd called home, but no luck. Then we heard an announcement over the loudspeaker, "Would Mr. Gil Hill please come to the ticket booth. We have a boy that's lost, and one of the football players is holding him." I wanted to blister his butt for straying from us, but was so glad to see he was okay, I soon dismissed that idea. Not that I didn't have to do that on a number of other occasions.

Dennis was always an accident waiting to happen. He fell down the stairs in the home the church provided and broke his collar bone. He and his brother were riding down the steep hill on Jackson Street on a bicycle, and Dennis was on the handle bars. At the bottom of the hill, he went head first onto the sidewalk. David brought him home with his face looking like raw hamburger. Melva called me to come home, and we patched his face up best we could before taking him to a doctor. The stitches left a visible scar!

One day, Melva said to me, "I was visiting the lady next door, and she said they go to a church that speaks in tongues." Then Melva said, "I don't think she meant the kind of tongues I've heard him using on the dog out back!"

Pam started high school from there, and had to ride the bus to Pittman. Not sure of the occasion, but she had her first date that year. When she came home, I asked how it went, and she said, "Oh, we really made out!"

"Whoops! Sit down, girl; explain that to me." Well, it didn't mean at all what I thought it meant; just teenage language for "we had a good time."

It was time to move again. We bought a house in Eastwood Hills, using my veteran's claim, and we moved during the summer of 1966. We were still seeking God's direction for our lives as we continued to serve Hollywood Church on a part-time basis.

Next up? Becoming a Presbyterian!!

Chapter 19

EASTWOOD HILLS

A fter getting the children enrolled in new schools, we settled down in a new home with our dogs. Think I forgot to mention that while living on Spruce, we bought our first dog, a beagle. We named her Samantha! Although we had a fenced in backyard, Samantha found a way to let a male mutt in the yard while she was in heat, and do his number on her. After she had puppies, we gave them away, except for one with a deformed foot, which we kept and named Whimpie!

The home in Eastwood had a basement, and I'd just finished painting the hallway leading down stairs, when Samantha decided to scrounge under the dinner table for scraps. I opened the door to the downstairs and gave her orders to get down there. When she hesitated, I gave her a little shove with my foot and closed the door. The door cut off the tip of her tail, so down the stairs she went, throwing blood all over both sides of the new paint job! I'm not sure whether Melva and the kids laughed or cried, but I know I had to paint the hallway again!

At this point in time, I was driving 10 miles, one way, to the church office at Hollywood. I desperately needed a different car because the other one conked out, so found a small white Volvo for $500.

～

While in the seminary, a neighbor had informed me about a farmer he knew who had a bass pond, and might let us go fishing there. Whenever I had any spare time, which was seldom, I took the boys to the pond, and taught them how to fish. We usually used minnows with great success, so, one day, we were coming home with the minnow pail on the floorboard of the car, filled with fish, when Dennis proceeded to dump the pail over. I wasn't too happy, and it took months to get the fish smell out of the car.

Another time, I placed my contact lens on the open door of the glove compartment, and Dennis got in the car, and shut the door. I found one contact lens, but the other one was gone.

I enrolled the boys in Little League Baseball, and Dennis was playing catch in the front yard with a neighbor, when the ball goes through his glove, and hits him in the eye. The result was a real shiner! Later in life, he said, "Dad, don't you remember any good things about me?"

One day, I'm at the church, when the phone rings, and the conversation goes something like this, "Mr. Hill, a friend gave me your name, and I'd like to get married." After determining who the friend was, and that the caller had a distinct accent, I responded, "If you and your lady will come to my office, we'll have you fill out some papers, go through some counseling, and decide if I want to marry you." There was dead silence on his end of the line, until he says, "Hey, man, all I vant to do is get married!" He hung up, and I missed my chance to do my first wedding. Thinking back, I wasn't licensed then anyway.

In the fall of 1966, the pastor of South Presbyterian Church, whom I'd met at a Presbytery meeting, called and said he'd like to visit with me. We had a meeting over lunch, where he asked me if I'd be interested in joining his staff, as an assistant, with an emphasis on evangelism and visitation.

After we prayed about it, Melva and I decided it was another door God had opened, and we made plans to go there. On Sunday, I announced it to those we loved at Hollywood. Goodbyes are never easy, but they sent us on with God's blessings and gratitude for our time together. I met with the Presbytery, which is Presbyterian protocol, and they agreed; although some had reservations about my Baptist background.

Here we go again! Stay tuned!

Chapter 20

SOUTH PRESBYTERIAN CHURCH

In 1967, I began making the 20 mile journey from Eastwood Hills to South Presbyterian Church at 75th and Holmes in Kansas City, five days a week, with Monday and Saturday off. Melva soon joined the choir and made the trip with me on nights she had practice. Pam was old enough to be with the boys while we were both gone, and we settled into another routine.

We soon met a couple there, Gerald and Harlene Scofield, who became good friends. Gerald and I had a common interest in athletics. Harlene played the organ, so she and Melva enjoyed a musical interest. They had two daughters Pam's age, so she had new friends also.

Six months after ministry at South, a commission was formed including members of the Presbytery and church elders. With my family and a few church members there, I was ordained a Presbyterian minister on the July ninth, 1967.

My days were spent out in the neighborhood calling on those who had visited the church. On Sundays, I assisted the pastor, Joe Ledford, in the services by leading in prayers, reading scripture, or making announcements. On a few occasions, I had the opportunity to give the sermon.

After a Sunday service, when I introduced members of FCA as speakers, Joe called me into his office and put the word "athletics" before me. He asked me to pronounce it. I said, as I always had, "ath-e-le-tics," pronouncing it as a four syllable word. He corrected me and, to this day, I always say, "Athlete, athletics!" Joe had a local radio program and was a stickler for correct English.

For recreation, I joined a nearby Jewish Community Center. That's where James Jeffrey taught me how to play handball. It wasn't much fun playing him because he had been a star in football and other sports in the military and at Baylor. In a handball game, where you play to 15, he'd beat me by 13 points. I don't remember ever winning. However, after his many lessons, I entered a tournament of class C players and managed to hold my own. Jeff and I also found time for golf and our families shared meals on occasion.

I attended a couple FCA camps, which were very inspirational. At the camps, we would meet daily in huddle groups for prayer and sharing the gospel, after which we'd take part in athletic games. Each evening, famous people from the sports world would share their Christian Testimony and Ray would lead us in uplifting songs in the assembly hall.

While at South, a local funeral home called needing someone to conduct a funeral. The church secretary forwarded the call to me. I did that funeral and subsequently served the funeral home for many other funerals where a minister was needed. I never realized until then how many people die without benefit of clergy, or without a religious ceremony. I also learned that some funerals have very few relatives or friends in attendance.

Sometime in 1968, Joe announced to the congregation that he was accepting a position as administrator of a new Presbyterian Retirement Home and would be leaving the church. I knew he had already been spending a lot of time on that project and wasn't surprised, but I was totally shaken to find out I would be the pastor of this big church while they were engaged in a senior pastor search.

My days were spent learning how to prepare a weekly message, moderate session meetings, keep the wheels of the church turning, and visit the sick and elderly. It was a great experience for almost a year, which was the time it usually takes a church to complete a new pastor search.

The church had a vacant lot out back, and I was instrumental in having a softball diamond erected in hopes it might bring some new kids to the church. We had a Boy-Scout troop that would regularly meet in the church, and it was put to use as their playground following their meetings.

I lived a busy life until the fall of 1969 when the church extended a call to Ed Gammon as pastor. I was told that, in the Presbyterian way, new pastors would prefer going it alone or building their own staff. That didn't mean, "You are fired!" It's a nice way of saying you should start looking for another place of service, which involved my completing a dossier and circulating it throughout the denomination.

Melva and I were fast asleep when I received a telephone call from a person in Clovis, New Mexico. He said, "We're in need of a minister and, having read your dossier, wanted to know if you'd come to Clovis for an interview." I turned to Melva, now wide awake, and said,

"Honey, would you like to go to Clovis?" She said, "Where in the world is that?"

WE SOON FOUND OUT!

Chapter 21

KANSAS CITY HIGHLIGHTS

Before leaving Kansas City, there are two highlights I'd like to mention.

The first one is what happened at a Kansas City Chiefs football game. In 1967, I was asked to give the prayer before one of their games; it's hard to believe that was once allowed. As people entered the stadium for the game, a heavy rain began to come down. When it came time for the prayer, I said a generic prayer about protecting the players from injury and keeping us safe as we return home. Then these unexpected words came out, "Now, God, if You will turn off the rain, we are ready to play football."

That brought a huge rumble from the crowd. However, as I walked to my seat in the stands, the rain stopped, and the people began clapping. I just kept walking hoping no one would recognize me.

The following day, the Kansas City papers ran this headline on the sports page, "LOCAL MINISTER TURNS OFF THE RAIN." I got a lot of ribbing from friends and a few phone calls from farmers asking me to turn the rain on.

The second highlight concerned a "Billy Graham Crusade" in Kansas City in 1968. I had been asked to be prayer chairman by the Ministerial Alliance. No, it didn't have anything to do with turning off the rain! When the members of the crusade team came to town, one of my duties was to provide a ride for them from the airport to their hotel. In doing so, I had the opportunity to meet Cliff Barrows and George Beverly Shea personally.

Prayer groups were organized throughout the city and God honored our prayers. The attendance at the crusade was in the thousands each night. Billy Graham preached his message, and, when the invitation was given, many people responded by walking down the aisles to accept Christ as their Savior.

"GOD IS GOOD ALL THE TIME. ALL THE TIME GOD IS GOOD!"

kansas city chiefs football club

5605 EAST 63RD TRAFFICWAY • KANSAS CITY, MISSOURI 64130 • AREA CODE 816 • 924-9300

Jack W. Steadman
Executive Vice President
and General Manager

July 23, 1968

Reverend Gil Hill
South Presbyterian Church
7850 Holmes Road
Kansas City, Missouri

Dear Reverend Hill:

We appreciate your bringing the invocation for our game with
the Denver Broncos this Saturday night, July 27. I am enclosing
your press box pass and five complimentary tickets for you and
your family.

The invocation is timed for 7:11 PM and should not exceed
45 seconds. Since you have done this for us before, I'm sure you
know what we have in mind. I would appreciate your reporting to
the P. A. announcers booth in the press box by 7:05 PM.

Hope you and your family enjoy the game.

Sincerely,

(Miss) Gerre Ann Sprague
Pre-game and Halftime Coordinator

The day I turned the rain off

LIFE IN CLOVIS, NEW MEXICO

I called the man back and told him I'd like to come to Clovis for a visit. After coordinating dates and times, I caught a plane from Kansas City to Amarillo, Texas, where two Westminster church members, Hubert and Gene met me.

My research told me that Clovis was on the eastern side of the state, just a few miles from the west Texas border. It was a thriving town of 30,000, mostly because Cannon Air Force Base was there. Farming, cattle feeding, and the railroad were the main industries.

After preaching at the church on Sunday, I met with the Pastor Nominating Committee. We parted with the understanding we'd both pray about the matter and let each other know of our decision. A few days after I returned to Kansas City, the chairperson of the committee called and said they had voted to invite me to be their pastor. Melva and I had already committed in prayer to accept if invited, so I accepted their invitation.

In the fall of 1969, we bought a used Rambler station wagon from a banker who was a member of South Church. We sold the house, sent our furniture ahead by van, and made the two day trip by car to Clovis. Pam was now a sophomore, David a sixth grader, and Dennis a fifth grader. At one point during the move, Pam said, "Dad, can we please stay there a while?" After she'd already moved eight times in her young life, I really couldn't blame her for asking!

The house we moved into, owned by the church, was a small, three-bedroom brick with a kitchen and two bathrooms. Prior to our moving, they made the one car garage part of the living room and added another bedroom and bath just off the kitchen. A small back yard was fenced in and adjacent to an alley. The address was 1008 West Christopher, and the street ended in a circle drive with our house on the north side of the circle. The schools were both within walking distance.

We soon made friends with our neighbors. After we invited a family who lived across the street to attend the church, they not only joined, but became part of some stories I'll be telling you about later.

Because it would take another book to write about all the many things that happened in our twelve years in Clovis, I'm going to put them under separate headings in this chapter.

HERE GOES! HELP ME LORD!

WESTMINSTER—BEGINNINGS

I asked Harry and Mona Pomeroy if they would prepare a brief history of Westminster's beginnings. Who better than the most faithful and dedicated church members I've ever known. Fifty-two charter members in the beginning, and now they are the only charter members still there. I believe they will be there until the church doors close or they graduate to Heaven.

Since they provided me with four pages of history, I'm taking the liberty to condense it for publication in this book. Here is some of the history they provided.

In 1964, First Presbyterian Clovis and Presbytery of the Southwest (PCUSA) made a survey of Clovis and determined there was room for another Presbyterian church. First Presbyterian church members and the Presbytery provided financial help and property was purchased at 31st and Thornton in northwest Clovis.

A steering committee was appointed, and Charles E. Somerville, Jr. was appointed by the Presbytery to be the organizing pastor. He and his wife, Ramona, found housing at 1008 W. Christopher. The work began with no building, no officers, no organization, no equipment, and no sense of direction, only willing people and lots of prayers.

The work of the committee was to organize and supervise church activities, set up a program of evangelistic visitation, prepare a budget; and schedule a long-range program. The Presbytery was picking up the pastor's salary and housing. Members of the church were mostly young married couples with children; therefore, they felt overwhelmed by the budget suggested. However, they took a leap of faith and moved on with the plans.

Looking for a place to meet, they found a church-like building, complete with an organ, pews, meeting rooms and carpeted floors on the corner of Prince and Manana. At the time, it was called "Chapel of Memories," known today as "Steed-Todd Mortuary." Yep, they began in a funeral home! Since it was also open for business on Sundays, they sometimes had to schedule around a viewing or a funeral. Their first church service at Steed-Todd was on Sunday, October

18, 1964. Fortunately, their children didn't find the casket room until the next to last Sunday there. They heard later that one of the young lads climbed into a casket to check out how it felt.

On Sunday, January 31, 1965, the church was formally organized. Charles Somerville, Jr. was called as the first pastor. Forty out of 52 charter members were present, and a session was elected. One person remarked it was the youngest session she had ever seen since no one was over 40 years old.

A building committee of six members was appointed on May 16, 1965. A loan and gifts provided the money and ground-breaking ceremonies were held on July 9, 1967.

First use of the new building was on January 14, 1968. The sanctuary was a large, hexagonal room divided by a temporary wall. Three classrooms, two restrooms, a pastor's study, and an efficiency kitchen in the hallway completed the building.

Chuck Somerville left in August 1969, and the church began looking for a pastor. A pulpit nominating committee was formed, and they contacted me in the fall of that year.

Don't close the book until you hear the rest of the story! Exciting things were about to happen in my life and at that little church Andy Christensen called "the snow-cone."

*"And we know that in all things God works
for the good of those who love Him, who
have been called according to His purpose."*
Romans 8:28

WESTMINSTER—THE CHALLENGE

It didn't take long to find out that God had led me to an unusual mission field. I soon learned that Clovis had over 40 churches of various denominations, and our little church would have difficulty growing where it had been built. We were in the northwestern part of town, and most of the new development was being built in the northeastern part of town.

I also found out that some of the charter members had returned to First Presbyterian and others had moved away for various reasons. I had discovered that because Clovis was a military town, people went out the back door as fast as we could get them in the front door, so to speak!

But I accepted the challenge and began with those God had placed under my care.

It has been said that you will find four kinds of people in churches, and I have found them in every church I've served. They are the "dedicated," the "debaters," the "drop-ins," and the "drop-outs."

The dedicated are there rain or shine, good times or bad times, always faithful, always can be counted on to do the work of the church. The debaters are those who debate whether or not to get involved in the church and whether or not to attend on a given Sunday. The drop-ins are the Easter, Christmas, and a few Sundays in between church folks. And, of course, the drop-outs have gone elsewhere or nowhere, looking for whatever they think will meet their needs. I've heard them called "church-hoppers" rather than "grasshoppers."

The most dedicated couple I've met in fifty years of ministry are still at Westminster Presbyterian Church. As I said before, Harry and Mona Pomeroy will be there until the church closes or God calls them home. Both of them worked for the Clovis Public Schools until retirement. Harry continues to teach at the Clovis Community College. On different dates, I had the privilege of officiating at the weddings of their two daughters. We have shared a meal on many occasions, and I visit with them every time I'm back in Clovis. They are my friends!

Shortly after arriving in Clovis, I joined the Curry County Ministerial Alliance. While there, I met the Reverend, now Bishop, Charles Green, pastor of the Church of God in Christ. We hunted pheasants together; we went to the Holy Land together; we had joint services with the two congregations; we prayed together. We have cried together over the deaths of our wives, Angie and Melva. Charles has been the dedicated pastor of the same church for over 60 years. Although in failing health due to a fall, he is still keeping on, keeping on! We break bread and spend time together whenever I'm back in Clovis! He is my brother-in-Christ and my friend!

WESTMINSTER—ME A PASTOR!

On Sunday, March 9, 1969, I was installed as pastor of Westminster Presbyterian Church in Clovis, New Mexico.

It was a long journey, and yet God had been leading all the way. From a young boy in Chadron, Nebraska, to becoming a World War Navy veteran; to earning a college degree; to being a high school athletic coach and classroom teacher; to getting a job as a life insurance and investment salesman; to meeting Jesus Christ as my Savior at age 30; to answering God's call to ministry at 35; to earning a seminary degree; to being a supply preacher; to being an assistant minister; to being ordained to the gospel ministry; to living with a beautiful wife and three children – and now for the first time at age 43 to being called "pastor!" WHAT A TRIP!

All of life had prepared me for this moment, though I had no idea what being called a pastor actually meant. Neither college nor seminary offered a class on the subject. It was trial and error, on the job training, a daily experience of working with all that goes on in a church environment. It was praying with and for people, rejoicing with those who were rejoicing, and crying with those who were crying. It was always asking for Holy Spirit counseling and guidance.

I found that some would call you "reverend;" some would call you "preacher;" some would call you "Gil;" some would call you "Mr. Hill," but only after you had earned it, would someone call you, "my pastor." And glory be to God, it sometimes happened as you can read in the letters following.

WESTMINSTER—CURRY COUNTY CRISIS CENTER

I can't recall the date when Jim and Nina Thomas joined Westminster. Nina was working as a social worker, and, one day, she came by my office and asked me to help her start a Crisis Center for Clovis and the surrounding area.

She outlined a three-fold objective for a telephone call-in service for those in crisis. A trained person would listen, help the caller resolve their crisis, and, if needed, refer them for professional help. Of course, there wasn't to be any personal contact or exchange of names.

I prayed about the matter, and, in a week or so, told her I would help. We lined up some board members, mainly Bob Brooks, the hospital administrator at the time, and Fred Tharp, an attorney friend. We secured funding through the United Way, trained some volunteers, and started the Crisis Center. We posted the phone number around town at places where it might be noticed and in phone booths. We also took out an ad to run daily in the local paper.

As director, my job was to train the volunteers and hold weekly meetings to discuss our service and the calls we'd received. On occasion, it would be necessary for me to take calls. Sometimes I would meet the caller at a designated time and place, but always with someone else accompanying me. The number of people who would call just to talk to someone never ceased to amaze me, and I thank God we were a friendly voice in their time of need.

During the twelve years I was in Clovis, we fielded hundreds of calls. Forty years later, and through many changes of personnel, the Crisis Center is still providing a valuable service to the community.

TO GOD BE THE GLORY!

WESTMINSTER—BUS TRIPS

A benefactor had given us a yellow school bus and we took two trips on it that were spiritual highs. The first was to Lubbock, Texas to hear Bill and Gloria Gaither when they were just getting started in gospel music. On the way, the bus broke down, and we had to get mechanical help to even get there. But we arrived on time and were thoroughly blessed by their music. Out of that concert came many of the songs we would later include in our own songbook.

The second trip was to Amarillo to a Kathryn Kuhlman healing service. A lady who accompanied us on the trip was healed of a stomach disorder at the service, and we saw many others touched by Kathryn's ministry that night. It was at this meeting where I first experienced the phenomena of "being slain in the spirit."

Kathryn had people line up for healing, and, when they would get close to her, she would ask them why they came. After hearing about their need, she'd say a prayer, hold out her hand, and over they would go into the arms of people called "catchers."

I remember one big cowboy who responded to her question about why he was in the line by saying, "My wife made me come because of a bad back." She asked him to touch his toes, but he couldn't even reach his knees, so she prayed for him, held out her hand, and over he went. After the catchers laid him down, he was immobile for a while. When he stood up, she asked him, "Do you feel anything?" Rather perplexed he said, "Why, what happened?" She then asked him to touch his toes, which he did easily, and then she had him twist and turn his back around to indicate it was better than before. He walked off the stage without any difficulty. Only God knows if the healing was permanent, but it certainly blessed me and many others who witnessed it that night.

I realize this might stretch your beliefs. At the time, it certainly did mine. But in many instances since that one I've seen God work in many wonderful ways, doing things that my human mind couldn't comprehend. Thus, I've come to believe He is a God of might and miracles. To all of them I only say, "To God Be the Glory, Great Things He Has Done."

I believe the greatest miracle of all is salvation, even though I had a seminary professor who said, "Technically, salvation isn't a miracle." Fifty plus years in the ministry and seeing hundreds come to know Him, I can only sing, "But when he saved my soul, cleansed and made me whole, it took a miracle of love and grace!"

WESTMINSTER—HIGH PLAINS CRUSADE FOR CHRIST

In 1972, I was serving as President of the Curry County Ministerial Alliance when I proposed we consider an evangelistic crusade for Clovis and the surrounding area. After discussion and prayer, it was agreed that we would contact Bill Glass, former Cleveland Brown professional football player, now an evangelist, to lead us.

We agreed with him on the dates of July 8 through July 15, 1973, and to call it "The High Plains Crusade for Christ." A steering committee of pastors and laymen was formed, a budget proposed, and work began with only eight months to get ready. Nazarene pastor Gerald Woods and I were asked to direct the effort. The Superintendent of Schools, a banker, and a realtor became members of the committee.

Money was raised, counselors were trained, and publicity began through the media. A choir was formed and some members of Westminster joined. We met for seven nights at the high school football stadium. Special music was offered along with testimonies from local Christians. Bill brought an evangelistic message each night ending with an invitation for people to respond by coming forward.

We were blessed by seeing many receive Christ for the first time and others renew their commitment to Him. I was personally blessed by seeing Cotton Hall, the neighbor I'd been praying for, make his decision to receive Christ. He later joined the church, and he and his family became life-long friends. He even took me, on another occasion, to visit his father, who was in an Amarillo hospital, and to pray for his dad's healing.

After his dad had returned home to Childress, Texas, Cotton called me and said, "My dad wants to measure you for a pair of hand-made boots." End result: a pair of ostrich skin boots. My first! God is full of surprises!

In the months following the crusade, I received nice letters from both Bill Glass and the Ministerial Alliance for my efforts concerning the crusade.

WESTMINSTER—CAMP CHIMNEY SPRINGS

Near Cloudcroft, New Mexico in the Sacramento Mountains, Presbyterians have a camp called Chimney Springs. We sent kids there from Westminster previously, but, in 1972, I was asked to direct the summer camp.

I recruited Gary and Jan Britt and a couple from Lubbock, Texas, to be camp counselors, and invited Tony and Shelby to lead the music. The campers included Charles Green's two girls and kids from Presbyterian churches in Lubbock, Texas, as well as kids from First Presbyterian, Clovis, and from our church.

We had a great time sharing God's goodness by the fireside, at meals, in small groups, and in a nightly gathering of singing, prayer, and worship. On the last night, we gave the campers an invitation to give their lives to Jesus, and many of the kids responded. I heard reports later, from those who had spent a week at the camp, who said the camp experience had changed their lives.

Another time, we were returning from camp on the back road leading to the highway to Roswell, when we saw an overturned motorcycle on the side of the road. A young man lay beside it, cut and bleeding. I learned later he had swerved to miss a rabbit and lost control of the motorcycle. When he hit the pavement, the visor on his helmet had shattered and cut his face badly. I stopped the car, rushed over, picked his head up, and my first words were, "Lord, we need your help here!"

Within a few seconds, a pick-up pulling a camper stopped, and a lady came running over, saying, "I'm a nurse; can I help?" She got the bleeding stopped and bandaged the cuts. We placed the boy on the bed in her camper, the motorcycle in the pick-up, and off they went to the hospital in Roswell.

I'm blessed to report that after taking my carload of campers back to Clovis, I returned to Roswell the next day to find the boy recovering and grateful for our help. I was able to lead him to the Lord in that hospital room as we thanked the Lord for saving his life, both physically and spiritually.

WESTMINSTER—THE GOSPEL GOES TO PRISON!

On the weekend of September 6-8, 1974, 15 to 18 other counselors and I were part of a Bill Glass Prison Ministry team at Santa Fe Penitentiary, New Mexico. This is a maximum-security prison, so we prayed continually for divine protection. As a result we didn't experience any problems while there.

Members of the team consisted of Bill, who played professional football for the Cleveland Browns; Mike Crain, a black belt karate expert; Paul Anderson, an Olympic gold medal winner in weight lifting; John Westbrook, a former professional football player with the Cincinnati Bengals; ventriloquist Ann Fairchild; McCoy McLemore, who played for the NBA World Champion Milwaukee Bucks; Bunny Martin, world's yo-yo champion; and J.C. Power Outlet, the musical group who led the music.

We were in the prison from 3:30 am to lock-down at 7:00 pm on Friday, 9:00 am to lock-down at 7:00 pm on Saturday and 11:00 am to 3:30 pm on Sunday. Our sleeping quarters were in a nearby motel. It was my first and last time in a prison. It was reassuring to know that when the prison doors opened we were free to go in and out!

We ate with the prisoners and had a chance to share our faith one-on-one when opportunity presented itself. I was able to play pool with some of the inmates and I became someone they would talk with after they saw my skill at eight-ball. I never realized until then that all those hours spent in the pool halls would someday be helpful in a prison ministry. I was blessed to counsel an inmate, Eddie Wiggins, who gave his heart to the Lord during our time there. He became a mail correspondent after I returned to Clovis. However, I lost contact with him after I moved to Nebraska. I'm wondering today if he's still alive.

Many of the inmates signed a letter thanking us for taking the time to share our faith with them. As is usually the case, we were the ones who experienced life-changing blessings during our days in prison.

WESTMINSTER—BLESSINGS KEPT COMING

One Sunday, while we were still in the divided sanctuary, a group of "hippies" walked in mid-service. It seems that Stanley Cole, a railroader who had a ministry to street kids, had told them about us, and they came to check us out.

Every eye turned their way, so I just said, "Welcome," and went on preaching. After the service, I got acquainted with Duke White, their leader, and a young lady whose name I don't recall. I invited them to return, but they never did. However, I met with a number of them at their downtown location and later met two boys,

Tony and Shelby, who sang and played the guitar, who would have an influence on lives at our Christian Camp.

The Lay Witness Movement was abroad in the land when we invited a team from West Texas to come and share their testimonies with us. It was the beginning of a number of changed lives as some of our members started going on other Lay Witness Missions and sharing their testimony.

I remember, during the Lay Witness mission, when the invitation was given to receive Christ, a member of Westminster, Hubert, said, "I've been a church member for years, but I don't know the man, Jesus." He made a profession of faith, and others followed him that day. Our church was on the move, and God was blessing us with increased growth and blessed lives.

Because the divided sanctuary only had seating for 50, we soon found ourselves needing to tear down the wall that divided the sanctuary. So, on a Sunday afternoon, "the wall came tumbling down." That provided comfortable space for at least 200, and we began to use it in many ways. The pulpit, the communion table, the baptism font, and the piano were moved to the end of the sanctuary, opposite the front door.

Since the area was to be a multi-purpose room, we ordered chairs instead of pews with a rack behind each chair for hymnals, a book of spiritual songs, and a registration pad. The pad is a sneaky way to find out who wasn't there on Sunday, but also to have a list of visitors so we could call on them in the week following.

I'd heard about a lady in Roswell, New Mexico, who liked to help churches with their musical needs. So, one day, I drove the 110 miles to Roswell, knocked on her door, stated who I was, and explained our need for an organ. She said she'd think about it. Less than a week later, a music store downtown said they had an organ for us and asked when we wanted it delivered. Now God would have to supply someone to play it, and He did! Many times!

The enlarged space with movable chairs enabled us to do a number of different things, like communion with the table in the center and everyone seated around it, or sitting in a circle and passing the communion elements to each other, putting the chairs facing the front door and having a guest evangelist sing from there, putting the chairs against the wall and having a dance! Well, I thought about that last one, but didn't do it! We did have a "foot-washing" on occasion though.

A number of military families were now attending the church: Ron and Janet Syrcle, Gary and Shelia Engel, Andy and Suzanne Christensen, Gary and Jan Britt, Steve and Kathy Altick, Bill and Judy Murray. There were those who were in Clovis working or teaching school: Rich and Eileen Koskie, Jim and Betty Hunsucker, George and Becky Esslinger, David and Sandy Miller, Elgin and Shirley Mallory, Bobby and Sharon Jordan, Bill and Thala Stalls, Mel and Lonna Kay Mapes, Mort and Bonnie Cross, Roy and Wilma Ploudre, Rick and Kathy Trask, Ray and Betty Eskridge, and our neighbors, Cotton and Barbara Hall. Others drove the 20 miles from Portales to worship with us: Chris and Betty Ingle, Otis and Sue Davis, Hubert and Donda Morgan, and a few others. We were blessed with visitors almost every Sunday. The children of our members, too numerous to mention, added to the joys of a Sunday morning. A complete record of baptisms and marriages was kept and is on file.

Speaking of baptism, from time to time, someone would request baptism by immersion. On those occasions, we'd use the baptistery of the Christian Church. It was always a blessing for those being baptized, for those in attendance, and for me. I still used the font at church for children and, any others who professed Christ and wanted to be baptized, by sprinkling. Someone once asked a Presbyterian pastor why they baptized that way and he said, "We believe a little dab will do you!"

Another story about that subject goes like this: A Baptist said to a Presbyterian, "You don't really baptize in the way Jesus taught, you know." To which the Presbyterian said: "If I got you wet up to your knees, would that count?" "No way," said the Baptist. "If I baptized you up to your chin would that count?" asked the Presbyterian. "Of course not," said the Baptist. "How about if I baptized all but the top of your head?" asked the Presbyterian. "Nope, you gotta do the top of the head," said the Baptist.

"That's exactly what we do," said the Presbyterian. And if you aren't laughing, you are probably a "fundie"!

Of course, the marriages I remember best were when I married two of my children while at Westminster, Gary Hamilton and Pam on February 13, 1972, and David and Jeannie Morris on January 25, 1976.

With Pam, I had the privilege only afforded to a very few men: to walk your daughter down the aisle, give her to another man, and then officiate at her wedding. Melva wept, and I kept my composure the best I could, until after the ceremony was over! Among the greatest joys of my life is to have officiated at the wedding of my three children and three of my grandchildren.

WESTMINSTER—MORE BLESSINGS

After our first Lay Witness Mission we started (PTL) Praise the Lord groups meeting on Tuesday and Thursday nights in members' homes. Usually six to eight people would come together for singing, praying, and the study of God's Word, with the host being the leader. What a blessing they were as people shared their joys and their sorrows, prayed for one another and for others, and gained a new understanding of the Scriptures.

Out of that came a Wednesday morning Bible Study at the church, which Melva and I led, and ladies from Westminster and other churches attended. Sometimes we had a guitarist, but mostly the singing was a cappella. I never tried to lead the singing because when I sang, people knew why I was called to preach!

On one occasion, we elected the youngest elder in the history of the Presbyterian Church. Chuck Jones, son of Buddy and Betty Jones, was only 18 at the time, but a very mature young man. I understand that, after college, he became a Christian educator.

From time to time, our elders on session had some "heavy issues" to deal with, but we had a standing rule—unless we were all in agreement, nothing would be done about the issue until it appeared on the docket again.

When I first arrived at Westminster, the average age of the congregation was 35, and I was a senior at 43. Over the years, that average moved up as people of all ages joined us.

Of course, like all churches, we had numerous fellowship dinners (some call them pot-lucks)! That's because when everyone brings a pot you take some food out of each pot, hoping you'll get lucky, and it will tickle your pallet. Melva's potato salad was a hit and always went fast. Just ask Steve Altick!

We experienced many spiritual miracles: the healing of bodies, the healing of marriages, and eternity healings for those who found Jesus as Savior.

Jan Britt reminded me of a young man named Jay, who came to one of our healing services with a bad back, and, after prayer, laying on of hands and anointing with oil, he was able to take the brace off his back and go running towards home. Do healing miracles happen all the time? No, but, when they do, I believe you give glory to God and keep on believing that Jesus still gives sight to the blind and causes the lame to walk again.

WESTMINSTER—U.S. BICENTENNIAL YEAR—1976

We did a few things to make the year special and one we wouldn't soon forget.

I began a radio program at a Christian station out of Farwell, Texas, entitled, "God Bless America Again," with a daily 10 minute talk on America's heritage and the need for God. Two businessmen friends sponsored the program.

I had our Volkswagen Bus painted with the theme "God Bless America Again," in bright red, white, and blue colors. It got a lot of attention as I drove up and down Main Street. I even heard remarks such as, "There goes that crazy preacher."

The bus had been provided by Leslie Pattison, a member of First Presbyterian, who liked to help us financially from time to time. When I told him I'd like to start a cassette tape ministry for all the military folks who'd been through Westminster and were scattered abroad in the land, he provided the funds.

I bought a high speed tape duplicator which could duplicate a 20 minute sermon in 3-4 minutes.

Each week, we would make copies of the Sunday sermon and send them out. One day, Leslie came to see me, and I showed him what we were doing with the equipment he provided. I said, "We put a 20 minute sermon on tape, and the machine gives you a recording of it in 3-4 minutes." Leslie, in all innocence, said, "You mean it boils it down to that!" Everyone has probably heard a number of 20-30 minute sermons they'd like to boil down to 3-4 minutes. I know I have, and that's why I always tried to limit sermons to 20 minutes!

I truly believe that our nation has turned its back on God in many ways and unless He blesses us again, we'll ultimately destroy ourselves like the other great nations have destroyed themselves. God's word says in 2 Chronicles 7:14, "if my people, who are called by name, will humble themselves and pray and seek my face and turn from their wicked ways, then I will hear from Heaven and will forgive their sin and heal their land." PRAY WITH ME, GOD BLESS AMERICA AGAIN!

WESTMINSTER—THE DOVE

God sent Noah a dove to signify the flood was over. He sent us a dove without a clear sign as to what it meant.

We had finished the third phase of a building program, which included a kitchen, fellowship hall, and a pastor and secretary office. Melva and I were on the floor of the secretary's office, putting some pictures into frames when a dove walked in!

The date written on the back of the picture of a dove lighting on the branch of a tree just below a waterfall of sparkling blue water is August 29, 1978. Here's what I wrote on the back of the picture, "Today, at about 9:30am, while preparing this picture for framing, I was on my knees on the floor of the secretarial office. Melva was on her knees preparing another picture for framing, when a beautiful white dove walked into the office." Both the door to the fellowship hall and the door to the office were slightly open because of a very warm day which allowed the bird access.

After getting over the initial shock of seeing a bird, I held out my finger and the bird hopped on it. Wondering what this sign from God meant, we decided to keep the dove, called a friend to bring us a bird cage, and took the bird home with us for safe-keeping. We decided to call the dove JOY.

I also wrote these words on the back of the picture: "Thank you, Heavenly Father. Thank you, Jesus. Thank you, Holy Spirit for this sign and this wonder."

I didn't realize it at the time, but later events led us to believe that the sign was the first of many, telling us our work at Westminster was winding down, and it would soon be time to move again.

Joy accompanied us to our next field of service in Fairfield, Nebraska, where she died on August 27, 1984. It was almost six years to the date when she came to live with us. Melva was taking treatments for cancer at the time, and I wrote on the back of the picture: "Thank you, Jesus. Thank you, Heavenly Father. Thank you, Holy Spirit for Melva's healing. Thank you for sending JOY to live with us! Amen!

Shortly thereafter, we received a call from Melva's doctor saying the cancer was in remission. A year later, however, the cancer returned and claimed her life. Was the death of JOY another sign of what was to come? Only God knows, but I've long ago stopped believing in coincidences!

Both Melva and Joy have been committed to God, and, therefore, "I know in whom I have believed, and I am persuaded, He is able to keep that which I've committed unto Him against that day." 2 Timothy 1:12

WESTMINSTER—1969-1981

During the years I was a pastor of the church, we were a "take them in and send them out" church.

Mostly because we were serving young families and military families on the move. However, God was gracious and always seemed to send someone to take the place of those who were leaving.

In the early '70s, the "Charismatic Movement" came to Westminster. It was a good thing when understood, but a divisive thing when misunderstood. From the Bible, the word "charismata" is from "charis" meaning "joy" and "mata" meaning "gifts." It has reference to 1 Corinthians 12:1-14 concerning the Holy Spirit's Gifts.

Over the years, many came to us with the gift of music and used their gifts to God's glory. Early on, Cavita Dillon, Vicki Wall, and Lenora Hample played the organ. Then Jean O'Neill and Linda Woltjer filled that need. After them came Joanne Cook and Dixie Williams. Jerry Wichael as singer, pianist, and choir leader shared his gifts. Eileen Koskie and Betty Hunsucker also shared theirs. Gary Engel was our choir director from '74 to '78. He even got Mel Mapes and Bobby Jordan to play the guitar with him. Mary Fechter played the organ often from '76 until '81, and Louise Renshaw played some in 1980. Becky Esslinger and Sandy Miller were there whenever and wherever their guitars were needed.

Choir members were many, so I can't possibly remember them all. The one closest to my heart, sweet Melva, is now singing for Jesus in Heavenly places. Sufficient to say that the choir was always a blessing and, on one occasion, even wrote their own cantata.

The gift of administration was evident in our elders and deacons, as was the gift of operations in Steve Altick and Jerry Wichael, who led our two building programs. The gifts of miracles and healings were evident as people were saved, baptized, and grew in the faith. I'll always be grateful to Shelia Engel for four years of secretarial work. She is the best secretary I ever had! In fact, she is the only secretary I ever had at Westminster!

Unfortunately, when all of those good things were happening, the enemy did his level best to cause dissension. So there came a time when we began to divide into the "We have the spirit; you don't have the spirit" congregation.

I think this joke fits here: "Two inmates in a mental institution were asked why they were there. The first said, 'I'm here because I have a hole in my head!' When asked the same question, the second said, 'I'm here because I have two holes in my head!' The first inmate turned to everyone and said, 'I can't stand those holier than thou people!'"

In time, some members of Westminster no longer felt they were a part of the church and left. I know I began providing ministry and messages that fed one group more than the other, and, for that, I'm asking those I failed for their forgiveness. Be assured, I've gone to God about it many times.

It was an experience that made me a better minister because I didn't make the same mistake in the other churches I served after leaving Westminster. I'm still a "Presbycostal," i.e. a Presbyterian filled with the Holy Spirit, but one with enlightened understanding of what that means. All I can say to everyone who came through the doors of Westminster is, "G.I.L. LOVED YOU THEN AND G.I.L. LOVES YOU NOW!"

WESTMINSTER—TIME TO MOVE AGAIN!

In the summer of 1979, Melva and I booked a plane to Los Angeles to attend a Clyde Narramore seminar on Church growth. When we returned, I was told about some things that had taken place in my absence, which led me to believe it was time for a change. No one was pushing me out the door, but the handwriting was on the wall. Not only that, we were experiencing the "empty nest syndrome" because our children had moved to jobs in other states.

So I updated my dossier and had the national office start sending it out to churches looking for a pastor. I interviewed at a church in Texas and another in Oklahoma. In Oklahoma, the pulpit committee noticed I had Nebraska roots and asked, "Who would you yell for on game day, Oklahoma or Nebraska?" I responded, "Big Red, of course!" For those of you who don't know the school colors, they are both red! I guess they didn't like my smart-aleck answer because I never heard from them again. In January 1981, I received a call from the chairperson of the pulpit committee in Fairfield, Nebraska. She asked me to come to Fairfield for an interview. After praying about it, Melva and I decided to make the trip. It also meant I could visit my parents in Lincoln during the same time.

We spent our first night in Liberal, Kansas. The next day, we had a flat tire, which made us late to meet the committee in Fairfield. Not a good beginning, but they were gracious and the interview went well.

We discovered the Fairfield Community Church was the only church in a farm community of 300 and was a merger of a Methodist and

Christian Church who opted to become Presbyterians. The church building was of brick construction with a sanctuary seating 200, a fellowship hall and kitchen, a parlor, two offices, and three Church School classrooms.

A nice, two-bedroom manse with an office, living room, kitchen, full basement, and two car garage sat on a corner just northwest of the church.

We left that day feeling good about the situation. The members of the committee and Melva and I stated we would commit the matter to the Lord.

After we returned to Clovis, Ardyce Barnett, the chairperson of the pulpit committee, called and said they would like to come to Clovis on a Sunday to hear me preach and to visit again. Subsequently, four people from Fairfield were at Westminster, posing as friends from Nebraska. Over lunch that day, they asked if we would like to come to Fairfield. We said yes and asked for time to notify the congregation at Westminster before making the move.

How do you say goodbye to people you love and people who love you? Because our children had already moved from Clovis, the decision was a little easier. Also, the Alticks, Britts, Engels, Koskies, Syrcles and others had left Clovis.

However, most of those remaining were people I'd rejoiced with and cried with. I'd baptized many of them and their children, and seen them mature in their Christian faith. They had put up with my idiosyncrasies and helped me grow as a pastor. Saying goodbye was one of the hardest things I've ever done, but it was time. So we prepared to move back to Nebraska, to the state in which I was born and had spent the first 28 years of my life. Full circle? Time will tell!

WESTMINSTER—GOODBYE LETTERS!

Dear Brothers and Sisters in Christ:

The Community Presbyterian Church of Fairfield, Nebraska, has extended the call for me to be their pastor, and I have accepted effective May 1, 1981.

Over twelve years ago, you gave me the greatest privilege a man can receive. You called me to be your pastor! What a glorious time we have experienced together. Your cooperation, your support, and your love have made our ministry here a true joy.

Now the Lord is leading us to a new field of service. Because of our love for you, it hasn't been an easy decision. However, the Lord provided an open door; we pushed on it; it remained open; and now we must walk through it.

I will preach my last sermon at Westminster on Sunday, April 26, which means we only have three more Sundays to worship together. I'm believing you will want to be present.

As Melva and I leave Clovis, I am confident of four things:

This is God's will for us.

This is God's will for Westminster.

This is God's will for Fairfield.

This is God's will for the person He is preparing to be your next pastor.

Agape. You will be in our prayers. Please keep us in yours. Gil

DEARLY BELOVED IN CHRIST JESUS:

By the time you receive this newsletter, Melva and I will be on our way to Fairfield, Nebraska.

As most of you know, we have received the call to serve as pastor of the Fairfield Community Presbyterian Church beginning May 1, 1981.

We thank God for each of you who have supported us with your prayers, finances, encouragement, and abundant love during our years of fruitful ministry at Westminster. God has truly blessed us and to Him be the glory!

In a sense, we will be going home again! We will be living only 82 miles from Beatrice, where Melva and I were married 31 years ago, and only 100 miles from Lincoln, where I went to college and where my parents live.

Remember, God loves you, and I love you. See you in the end-zone! Gil.

Charismatic   Evangelical

Westminster Presbyterian Church
"A GROWING CHURCH SERVING GOD BY SERVING OTHERS"

PHONE 762-1217

7112 NORTH THORNTON   Clovis, New Mexico
88101

love   Joy   peace

YOU are invited to share the excitement we have found in Jesus Christ!

Sunday:
Bible Study for all ages . . . . 9:30 a.m.
Worship . . . . 10:45 a.m.
Youth Fellowship . . . . 5:00 p.m.
Praise The Lord . . . . 7:00 p.m.

Wednesday:
Bible Study . . . . 10:00 a.m.
Body Life groups . . . . 7:00 p.m.

Many other edifying times as scheduled

Spacious Nursery Provided For All Events

expect a miracle

Our Pastor — Gilbert L. Hill
"And His gifts were that some should be . . . pastors and teachers, for the equipping of the saints, for the work of ministry, for building up the body of Christ."   *Ephesians 4:11-12*

STATEMENT OF MISSION

Believing ourselves to be a church (the people of God — a part of The Body of Christ — and members in particular) we see our mission (our job) to be in relation to the "Great Commission" as set forth by our Lord in Matthew 28:18-20, where He says:
"Therefore, *GO* and *MAKE* disciples in all nations, *BAPTIZING* them in the name of the Father and the Son and the Holy Spirit, and then *TEACH* these new disciples to obey all the commands I have given you; . . . (Living Bible)

GOALS

1. To Glorify God in all we say and do
2. To proclaim Jesus Christ as Savior and Lord
3. To seek the fullness of the Holy Spirit and His gifts
4. To evangelize
5. To worship
6. To participate in the Sacraments
7. To teach and train disciples
8. To teach and practice good stewardship
9. To serve God by serving others

MINISTRIES of the body of Christ at Westminster:

. . . *Proclaiming the Good News (the Gospel) by word and deed*

. . . *Teaching God's Word (the Bible)*

. . . *Lending Library (including over 500 books and 100 cassette tapes)*

. . . *Tape Ministry (over 100 cassette tapes are mailed monthly to people around the world)*

. . . *Puppet Ministry (the Good News Puppets appear on TV3 weekly and are available for performances)*

. . . *Radio Ministry (God Bless America Again! with Gil Hill as speaker)*
KZOL Farwell at 7:10 a.m.
KENM Portales at 12:55 p.m.
KWKA Clovis at 12:45 p.m.

. . . *Music Ministry (our choir and congregation sing much of the music made popular by the Bill Gaither Trio)*

. . . *Healing Ministry (our elders are available for annointing with oil and prayer according to James 5:14-15)*

MINISTRIES which are supported by the body of Christ at Westminster:

LOCAL

The Crisis Center

The Salvation Army

Bruce's Home

Council on Alcoholism

The Girls club

Circle of Concern

Mental Retardation

United Fund

Pastor administered
HELP Fund

Soon Shil Sung — Our adopted daughter in Korea.

Tukidi — our adopted son in Indonesia.

AROUND THE WORLD

General Mission of the
United Presbyterian Church

Food For The Hungry

Bill Glass Prison Ministry

American Bible Society

Fellowship of Christian Athletes

World Literature Crusade

The Navigators

Billy Graham Evangelism

Vicki Kyte who is on the staff
of Campus Crusade for Christ

WE BELIEVE IN:

1. Man's sin (selfishness) *"For all have sinned and come short of the glory of God"* — Romans 3:23

2. God's grace (unmerited favor) *"For by grace are you saved, through faith, and not of yourselves, it is a gift of God."* — Ephesians 2:8

3. Christ's redemption (He died for us) *"In Him we have redemption through His blood."* — Ephesians 1:7

4. Holy Spirit fullness (controlled and empowered by) *". . . but be filled with the Spirit."* — Ephesians 5:18

5. The Gifts of the Spirit (for edification of the body of Christ) — I Corinthians 12, 13, and 14

6. The Fruits of the Spirit (which are being produced in a Spirit-filled life) — Galatians 5:22-23

7. The Return of Our Lord (for His Church) *"Behold, he comes . . . ; and every eye shall see Him."* — Revelation 1:7

We Know Something Good About

Gil —

You are so thoughtful, concerning my problems!
Jan

Your love & care for others
You give of your time, etc. Melva

You are _you_ and so unique — I love you — Thala

The amount of time spent keeping up with your flock and caring about their cares is truly noticed and appreciated. Your home visits are so important
Thank-you
Lynn

Your smiles say everything . . .
Mattie

I love you Gil + I appreciate how you can be such a "real friend" to me — Thank you for you — + I thank God for you Mary F.

You're a good listener, and a good
shepherd. Thank you for all you
do for all of us. Mona

Thank you for those poems you
leave for me in my car - You
always know when I need them..
Thanks for being you -
Agape you Janet

Thanks for being just a great father-in-law.
thanks for all the help. Jeannie

Most of all you are first a good
husband, a good father and a very
good minister
  agape - your sweet Rose.

Mother-in-law

THANK YOU

by JAN

THANK YOU FOR BEING YOU
  FOR ALWAYS UNDERSTANDING
FOR BEING HONESTLY CONCERNED
  AND NOT SO REPRIMANDING

THANK YOU FOR THE HOUR LONG TALKS
  ABOUT THIS-THAT-AND-THE-OTHER
AND DRAWING CLOSE WHEN I'VE BEEN DOWN
  LETTING ME CALL YOU BROTHER

THE SILLY GRIN, THE LOVE WITHIN
  THESE I NOW RECALL
THANK YOU FOR YOUR WITNESS
  TO ME, TO GOD, AND ALL

THANK YOU FOR DEALING WITH ME
  IN A GENTLE SORT OF WAY
TEACHING ME THE MEANING OF
  HOW IT FEELS TO AGAPE

THANK YOU FOR THE SIMPLE TRUTH
  OF GOD'S HOLY WORD YOU PREACH
THAT DRAWS US EACH A LITTLE CLOSER
  AND PUTS US IN HIS REACH

AND IT'S SO NICE TO KNOW, MY BROTHER
  WHEN YOU HAVE PROBLEMS, TOO
THAT YOU SOMETIMES WILL CALL ON ME
  AS I HAVE CALLED ON YOU

✝   ✝   ✝   ✝   ✝

THANK YOU, LORD, FOR GIVING TO ME
  A BROTHER WHO IS CLOSE TO THEE
HELP ME TO BE THE KIND OF FRIEND
  THAT GIL TO ME HAS ALWAYS BEEN

AMEN

Dear Bill,

In November I was called on to answer the following: "Describe a time when you were suddenly moved by a doctrine, bible verse or sermon and were subsequently changed." For me that happened in response to a sermon you preached all those years ago when you said something like "God is in the business of changing lives, and if your life has not been changed, you'd better examine your relationship with God." I point to that time as the beginning of my adult spiritual journey.

I was also deeply affected when I was next to ask you to direct the crisis center and your response was "I'll have to pray about that and let you know." I guess that was the first time in my life that someone indicated to me that prayer could be part of decision-making.

Those ten months in Crisis and our relationship with you during that time became a turning period in our lives. I have always believed that God sent us there for that reason. And so, in some small way, we have become two of those "missionaries" you used to speak of sending forth from Westminster Presbyterian.

And so in this holiday season, this note comes to say thank you for being who you are and for being such an important of our lives.

In love,
Fran

April 22, 1975

Dear Gil,

God _is_ Love – what a true
saying and so fitting for such
a brother as you. It's hard to
put into words what the past two
years have been for us, knowing
you.

I just thank God, that on this
day – you were born to become
our shepherd. It has been a
growing, learning and loving
experience and I look forward
to much more

I pray God's blessing for you and
your family; that the love of Jesus
will continue to flow from you –
to others!

Agape,
Sheila, Gary, John, Renee

Chapter 23

LIFE IN FAIRFIELD, NEBRASKA

I preached my last sermon at Westminster the last Sunday in April, 1981. The next month we rented a U-Haul, loaded our meager belongings and moved to Fairfield, Nebraska. Along the way, Melva turned to me and said, "Honey, Fairfield will be a fair field!"

The last year at Westminster had taken its toll on her peace of mind, more so than mine, because, where I had learned in athletics how to handle stress, she internalized everything. Perhaps that was one of the reasons we later had to deal with cancer in her life. In my reading of a book entitled, *The Causes and Cures for Cancer*, it clearly states that stress can be a contributing factor.

We began our ministry in Fairfield in June to a congregation comprised mostly of farmers or those in a business related to farming. The town had one grocery store, one restaurant, one gas station, one bank, and a post office. Everything was within walking distance, including a beautiful city park. A sand greens golf course was only a few miles away at Clay Center.

God knew we needed this place to be refreshed and renewed. The people welcomed us warmly and we soon settled in to our relaxed way of living. I even bought a bicycle and started making calls on my bike. I made friends with a teenager who lived near the church, and we often took bike rides together. Betty Juranek, a church member who lived a couple miles north of town, became my sounding board. I would ride out there once a week to have coffee, visit and talk about life in Fairfield.

The church was doing well with Elsie Broderick, a retired lady, as organist. Sonnie Fike helped with the music. Marion Fike became a good friend, and we soon were playing golf, racquetball, and hunting pheasants together. They both remain good friends in the Lord!

In the summer of 1983, Gary, my son-in-law, called and asked if Pam and the three kids could live with us while he was a traveling salesman. We, of course, said yes! Little did we know what an added blessing that would turn out to be. Shawn started school and found a new friend in Kip Kissinger. The city park became the playground for me and the kids. Hunting night crawlers with a flashlight was a new and exciting experience for them. Shannon even tried eating them, but didn't find them as appetizing as they looked. Seth liked the tire swing in our back yard and being with his grandma. They all three liked playing dress up at Mrs. Bienhoff's house, who everyone called Mrs. B.

Pam was there for a reason only God knew about! Melva hadn't been feeling well for quite some time, so, as I was getting ready to take a group to the Holy Land, we decided to have a physical exam so she could go with me. Our doctor in Hastings, Nebraska, thought it was probably a diseased gall-bladder that needed to come out and scheduled surgery. Pam and I were in the waiting room at the hospital in Hastings when the doctor came out and hit us with the word no one wants to hear: CANCER! Then he said it was wrapped around a major artery and was inoperable. What a blow to our serenity. What now?

We opted for a trip to the Omaha Med Center. There, after a thorough examination, they prescribed radium treatments which could be administered by an oncologist in Hastings.

That meant regular trips to the doctor, and lots of praying by us and the Fairfield congregation.

Pam and the kids stayed with us until school was out in May. Then they went back to Clovis to live in our house on Christopher. Gary took a sales job with Hagelgantz Ford, and Pam returned to her job at CAFB. I will always treasure those months with my grandchildren and daughter. We hated to see them leave, and the house wasn't the same without them there to come home to!

FAIRFIELD BLESSINGS—1981-1986

As He always does, God had us in the right place during this time in our lives. It went by fast, but these are some of the blessings I remember about Fairfield Presbyterian Church.

Don and Shirley Staires came into my life during a Lay Witness Mission at Westminster in Clovis, New Mexico. They had started a camp ministry in Oklahoma called "Shepherd's Fold," and I had visited there a couple times. So I proposed to the Fairfield Session that we invite them to hold a Lay Witness Mission at the Fairfield Church. They came in 1982 with a team of like-minded Christians and truly blessed those who were open to their witness. Of course, there were also those who didn't like people from Oklahoma coming to Nebraska and telling them how to live for Christ.

Shortly thereafter, Marion and Sonnie Fike took some of our youth to the camp in Oklahoma and came back with the Holy Spirit's urge to begin a camp on their farm. They named it "Manna Resort," and it has become the place where many young people have been led to Christ and had their faith renewed for over 25 years.

We began a Wednesday morning Bible Study like the one we'd started in Clovis. Soon we had ladies from the surrounding area gathering with some of our church members for an hour of fellowship and study on a weekly basis. Melva and I led the study until her declining health kept her from being with us.

We tried having a brown-bag lunch for the men at noon the same day, but found out that busy farmers just couldn't break up their days by coming to town for a Bible Study.

Our son Dennis came to live with us while we were at Fairfield. He soon found employment in Hastings and moved there. He was a tower of strength for me during his mother's illness and was there for me when she died. While in Hastings, he met Mary, who later became his wife.

I'm not sure I was the minister the people in Fairfield church needed during those years, but they were definitely the people I needed. They prayed for me and helped me go through the death of the most important person in my life. For that I will be eternally grateful!

LIFE IN FAIRFIELD—THIS 'N' THAT

Betty Peck, a member of the Fairfield Church, wrote a column for the weekly Clay County Newspaper. This is what she wrote on April 29, 1982.

A year ago this month, you may perhaps remember, I wrote a column about the gentleman from New Mexico presenting his credentials at a church service with a view to becoming our pastor. I believe I told you at that time that he was accepted by the congregation and only time would tell what we got, right? Well I thought you might like some follow-up on the matter since a lot can happen in a year.

Ours is a Community Church. Community Presbyterian Church, but I like to forget the Presbyterian.

To make a long story short, when a merger of the two churches in Fairfield at the time was suggested, they put the members of both churches in a sack, shook them up and out came Presbyterian. We had to call ourselves something in order to get a minister to serve us and I expect Presbyterian was probably as accurately describes what emerged as anything.

We have just the one church in town now and everyone is welcome there. We have open communion so no one is ever embarrassed by being passed over when communion is served. The church ministers to the needs of all families in the vicinity whether they ever brighten a pew with their presence or not. I think there is something magic in the words "Community Church." Long may it thrive.

Now to get back to the gentleman from New Mexico. First, I want to state that I have never been guilty of trying to make brownie points with anyone in my life. I say this in all honesty, because if I have, I wasn't aware of it. Second, we do have our differences. Wouldn't it be boring to see eye to eye all the time with anyone. Please remember this as I try to give you a bird's eye of the man who now fills our pulpit. I always have to smile when I hear the expression, "fills our pulpit." Sometimes the man up front seems to be dwarfed and others seem to stick out over the edges.

You remember in my earlier column I said, "I think we've got something." Well, now I KNOW it.

Our Sunday services have got something I've never encountered before. We are no longer simply observers, we are participants. Rather than sit through a sermon with our blessings and fears bottled up inside us we are encouraged to share them. Learning that you are not alone in your hopes and fears brings us closer to each other. We have become not only a growing but a caring church, and that is what it is all about, isn't it?

Our prayer chain is much used by many who feel the need for corporate prayer. We are learning to reach out both to give and receive. He teaches three separate groups of Bible study each Wednesday, A.M., P.M., and at noon. The attendance is fantastic with folks coming from other towns as well as the rural area. What a difference good leadership makes!

He has that very necessary thing, a sense of humor, and is not afraid to use it in the pulpit. If what we have, as Christians, is so good, why should we be long-faced about it? And there is variety in the services. Should you happen to be a guest in our church some Sunday, and you don't care for the service, come back next Sunday. Like Nebraska weather, it is bound to change.

He hasn't had Jonah swallowing the whale yet, but you never know. No, I'm being unfair. He never corrupts the Scriptures but gives them the realism that we can tie to our everyday living.

When he presented his credentials to be our Pastor, he didn't tell us about the beautiful woman he shares his life with, who tries to keep him in tune when he sings, and is tuned to our needs, always. But I guess even Pastors are entitled to have an ace up their sleeve upon occasion.

Fairfield Community Presbyterian Church, circa 1982

Chapter 24

HOLY LAND TOURS

In 1983, before we learned of Melva's cancer, I had been contacted by a pastor who was offering free trips to the Holy Land for any pastor who would put together a tour group of ten or more people. I put the word out and ended up with 17 people who wanted to go. Because Melva couldn't go, I invited my friend Charles Green from Clovis to go with us.

On June 15, 1983, the tour group took a plane out of Omaha to Israel, the place where Jesus began his ministry. Torn between concern for my wife and leading a group of people, I committed it all to the Lord and put on a good face of being in charge. We returned on June 24th with spiritual highs and pictures to share.

Charles was my stability and kept me going. On one occasion, we had undressed and put on swimming trunks to baptize each other and any members of our group who wanted to be baptized in the Jordan River. I'd laid my watch and billfold on a bench and was ready to walk out, when Charles said, "Gil, you can't do that! You have no assurance they'll be there when you come back." Of course he was right, and we found a more secure place for our valuables. What a blessing to be baptized in the Jordan and to have the privilege of baptizing others there. What an experience to visit where Jesus was born, where he walked while on earth, the Western Wall, Jerusalem, the Sea of Galilee, Gethsemane, the place where He was crucified and the empty tomb.

I was experiencing many of the things I'd been preaching about for the last 20 years. God had prepared me for this moment and so, "To God goes the glory, great things He has done, so loved He the world that He gave us His Son. Praise the Lord, Praise the Lord, let the earth hear His voice. Praise the Lord, Praise the Lord, let the people rejoice!"

While Melva's cancer was in remission, and so she could go, I put together a second Holy Land tour group. It included Ardyce Barnett and her mother from Fairfield and some college friends from Deshler, Nebraska. We joined another pastor and his group before flying out of New York on March 27, 1984 on Olympic Airways through Athens to Tel Aviv.

Here is the itinerary for the tour:

Wednesday, March 28. Welcome to Israel! Meeting and assistance by WHOLESALE TOURS INTERNATIONAL representatives and transfer to Tiberias for overnight at Hotel.

Thursday, March 29. Enjoy early morning boat ride on Sea of Galilee to Capernaum and visit ancient synagogue and St. Peter's House. Drive to Mt. of Beatitudes, Magdala, home of Mary Magdalene and Church. Return to hotel for of dinner and overnight stay.

Friday, March 30. Drive via Cana to Nazareth and visit Greek Orthodox Church with Mary's Well and Annunciation Chamber. Continue to Megiddo to visit excavations and tunnel. Then to Haifa and ascend Mt. Carmel for a magnificent view of city and harbor, Bahai Shrine and Persian Gardens. After lunch, drive to Caesarea and visit Roman Theatre and fortress. Return to hotel for dinner and overnight.

Saturday, March 31. Drive through the Jordan Valley to Jericho and visit ancient

Tel and view Mount of Temptation and Spring of Elisha. Continue to Qumran to view caves where Dead Sea Scrolls were found and then to Massada, last fortification of the Zealots in their war against Rome. Ascend by cable car to visit ruins of this famous Jewish fortress. Drive to Jerusalem for dinner and overnight at hotel.

Sunday, April 1. Drive via Mt. Scopus to Mt. of Olives for an outstanding view of Jerusalem and visit Chapel of Ascension. Descend to the Garden of Gethsemane and visit Church of All Nations. Proceed to Bethany and visit tomb of Lazarus. Then drive to Mt. Zion and visit the Upper Room and traditional Tomb of King David. Drive to the Holyland Hotel and visit model of Jerusalem in Herod's time. After lunch, drive to Bethlehem and view Shepherd's Field and visit Church of Nativity. Return to hotel for dinner and overnight.

Monday, April 2. Walk into the Old City. See St. Stephen's Gate, Pool of Bethesda and Chapel of Flagellation. Continue to Temple Mount viewing Dome of the Rock, El Aqsa Mosque and the Western Wall. Then on to Pilate's Judgement Hall with remains of Antonia Fortress, under Ecce

Homo and along Via Dolorosa to Church of Holy Sepulchre. Visit Garden Tomb with orientation beside Gordon's Calvary. Afternoon at leisure. Return to hotel for dinner and overnight.

Tuesday, April 3. Early morning departure back to New York.

If you are worn out reading about the tour, we were worn out doing it. It was especially hard on Melva; she had to spend time each day resting in her room at the hotels. She was a trooper, as always, but I could tell she didn't have the strength to really enjoy the trip. I'm glad we were able to make the trip together and I'm looking forward to reminiscing about it with her when I get to Heaven.

Pastor Charles Green at The Empty Tomb, 1983

Holy Land tour taken by 16 Clay Countians

Pastor Gilbert Hill and eleven members of Community Presbyterian Church returned June 24 from a 9 day tour of the Holy Land in Israel. The members of the church making the pilgrimage were Golden Ahlstrom, Vera Fuller, Opal Kriutzfield, LeVern and Vida Washburn, Marion and Sonnie Fike, Ron and Betty Juranek, Warren and Velda Wilson. Accompanying them from Fairfield were Marie Fike and Esther Spencer; from Harvard, Ernest and Ellamae Yost; and from Deshler, Betty Holle and Marion Vieselmeyer.

They left Fairfield June 15, drove to Omaha, and boarded a plane for New York, via Chicago. From New York they flew non-stop to Athens, Greece; then on to Tel Aviv, Israel, and Jerusalem where they joined 125 others taking the same tour.

Points of interest visited were Jericho, the Jordan River (where 9 members of the group were baptized), Tiberius and the Sea of Galilee, Mount of Beatitudes, Madgala (home of Mary Magdalene), Qumran (where the Dead Sea Scrolls were found), Masada, the Dead Sea, Jerusalem, Bethlehem, Mount of Olives, Gethsemane, the Garden Tomb, the Via Dolorosa, Pool of Bethesda, and many other sites.

In 9 days they traveled more than 15,000 miles and visited many historical sites, staying 2 nights in Tiberius, 5 in Jerusalem, and one in New York. They returned from Tel Aviv to Zurich, Switzerland, then to Geneva and back to New York.

If you have any interest in making a similar once in a lifetime journey please contact Pastor Hill at 726-2493 or write him at P.O. Box 187, Fairfield, 68938.

Ellamae Yost's description of the trip included the following information.

"As we were going to Egypt for two days we landed in Amman, Jordan and had the experience of Jordanian and Israeli customs at the Allenby Bridge which joins the two countries."

The group "visiting many of the Biblical sites in the Holy Land including Jericho, the River Jordan, Caesarea, Bethlehem, Nazareth, Jerusalem, the Garden Tomb beside Calvary where we participated in The Lord's Supper."

"(We) drove through the Jordan Valley to the Dead Sea where a few tried the "Dead Sea float". The caves where the Dead Sea Scrolls were found and took the cable car to Masada, the mountain fortress, but did not climb the additional 82 stairs to reach the top.

"We visited the Holocaust Museum in Jerusalem and the Shrine of the Book containing priceless Biblical scrolls.

"We then left our group and took an all day motorcoach drive from Jerusalem through part of the Sinai desert and crossed the Suez Canal by ferry and then to Cairo, Egypt. Had a sight seeing tour of the great pyramids of Giza and the Sphinx, had a camel ride and visited the Egyptian museum containing the treasures of King Tut."

Melva and Me overlooking Jerusalem, 1983

Chapter 25

MELVA'S DEATH

In the spring of 1984, Melva walked over to my office at church with the wonderful news from our doctor that her cancer was in remission. We relayed the news to our children, the congregation, and all our friends, with great rejoicing and thanking those who had been praying for her healing. We were asked to share about her healing in the local paper, and a writer from the Lincoln paper came out and interviewed us for a story.

However, in the fall of '84, the cancer returned with a vengeance. We ended up making her comfortable at home with hospice care out of Hastings. Pam and the children had returned to Clovis, and Dennis was managing a restaurant in Hastings. When members of the congregation would stop by to see her or bring us food, she always greeted them with a smile and asked them how they were doing. I had the difficult task of giving her pain shots on a regular basis, and we were alone in our bedroom when the Lord took her to Heaven on May 1, 1985.

Her body was donated to the Omaha Med Center and later cremated with the ashes returned to me. What I did then wouldn't work for everyone, but it was therapeutic for me to distribute a portion of her ashes where we met, where we were married, where we lived, where Pam was born, and some other places in Nebraska that were special only to us!

I invited a pastor, Dave Cornett, to help me with her Victory Celebration. It was held in the sanctuary at Fairfield with members of the congregation, our children, her mother, sister, and husband, and my sister and parents present. Although she had been set free from pain and suffering, I had great difficulty dealing with her dying at the age of 55 with so much to live for. I know all things work together for good to those who love God, but I'm looking forward to the time when I can sit at the feet of our Lord and have her death explained to me. I miss her and think about her almost every day!

A member of the congregation spoke these words as her epitaph, "Melva taught us how to live, and then she taught us how to die!"

Twenty years to the day, after her home going, I wrote a poem in her memory! A picture of Melva and me and our three children, taken on the occasion of our 25th wedding anniversary is included here.

August - 1975, 25th Wedding Anniversary
(Back) Pam and David (Front) Dennis, Melva, Me

Melva, her mother, Rose, and
her sister, Rose Marie

(Back) Melva, Me
(Front) Rose, Ward (my
dad), Dora (my mother)

MELVA

Twenty-years ago she went away
We've missed her each and every day.

She took up residence with God
And left us on this earthly sod.

Gone from us at age fifty-five
We've kept her legacy alive.

Devoted grandmother, mother and wife
Who put family first in her life.

Taught us about "agape love"
Unconditional, like our Father's above.

Sang about "Amazing Grace"
Always had a smile on her face.

Endured months of suffering and pain
It wasn't in her nature to complain.

Taught us how to live and how to die
So we can all meet in heaven by and by.

There to love, hug, and kiss as before
United in God's family forevermore.

Written by Gil Hill on May 1, 2005 for
Gary, Pam, Shawn, Seth and Shannon Hamilton
David, Jeannie and Clinton Hill
Dennis, Mary, Kent, Abbey, Madeline and Jack Hill

y News   -   May 9, 1985

Melva E. Hill

1929-1985

Melva E. Hill, 55, died May 1, 1985 at her home in Fairfield. At her request her body was donated to the Nebraska Anatomical Society for medical research with the remains to be cremated.

A memorial service of victory celebration was held in her honor Sunday, May 5 in Community Presbyterian Church of Fairfield with her husband, the Reverend Gilbert (Gil) Hill officiating, assisted by the Reverend David Cornett of Hastings and Don Staires.

Mrs. Hill was born Melva Elaine Clough to Milo and Rose Clough on October 3, 1929 in Beatrice and graduated from high school there in 1947 where she was football queen.

She and Mr. Hill were married in Beatrice on August 20, 1950 and lived in Table Rock and Blair, NE; Pueblo and Broomfield, CO; Kansas City, MO; and Clovis, NM before coming to Fairfield in May of 1981. She was a homemaker and mother, pastor's helpmate and gospel singer.

Her father preceded her in death. Among the survivors are her husband; her mother, Rose Clough and her sister, Rosie Bridgewater, both of Boulder, CO; one daughter, Pamela Hamilton, Clovis, NM; two sons, David, Greenville, TX and Dennis, Hastings; and 4 grandchildren.

Music was provided by Elsie Brodrick, organist, Sonnie Fike pianist, with vocal selections by her high school classmates, Pearleen and Virginia Jerman of Beatrice and by the church choir.

Memorials may be given to Fairfield Community Presbyterian Church or the American Cancer Society.

McLaughlin Funeral Home of Clay Center was in charge of local arrangements.

Me and Melva, circa 1984,
at home in Fairfield, Nebraska

Me at the pulpit at Gethsemane
Presbyterian Church, circa 2010

Chapter 26

LIFE AS AN INTERIM

For the first time in 35 years, I was living alone in a 3 bedroom house and learning again what it meant to be single. The Presbytery Executive paid me a visit and suggested my giving prayerful thought to interim ministry. In the meantime, I was still the pastor of the Fairfield Church.

In checking out interim ministry, I was told that you serve a church for approximately one year while they are searching for a minister to replace the one that has moved on. I was told there are three kinds of interims: those who keep the ship afloat, those who help the ship chart a new course, or those who sink the ship.

I believe this story about interims is worth telling here. A young lad was telling a friend they had an interim at his church, but when the friend asked, "What is an interim?" he said he'd have to ask his dad. The dad explained it this way, "Remember when we had a broken window in the house and put a piece of cardboard in it until we could have a new pane of glass installed? Well, that is kind of what an interim is: someone who takes the place of someone else for a while." So, the lad goes back to his friend and tells him he knows what an interim is. Then he says, "It's the person at the church who is filling in for the real pain!"

I was told the church in Kearney, Nebraska, was in need of an interim and would like me to apply. This I did, and, after an interview, they offered me the job beginning in the fall of 1986. I told the Fairfield church of my plans, and they let me go with their blessings. So, it was off to Kearney for a new beginning as a single man. Things went well there, and I didn't sink the ship while they were looking for a minister. In the fall of 1987, my interim there was over and I was asked to serve as interim at First Presbyterian, Fremont, Nebraska.

Ardyce Barnett was divorced, and we had been seeing each other since I left Fairfield. Yes, that's the same lady that was chairperson of the pulpit committee who interviewed me before I moved to Fairfield. We decided to get married in Grand Island and go to Fremont together. After less than a year, they called a minister, and we moved to Neosho, Missouri, as interim of the First Presbyterian Church there. My family from New Mexico and Texas came to visit us while in Neosho, and we spent fun time in Branson and at the Lake of the Ozarks seeing the shows and taking in the sights.

While in Fremont, Ardyce was still able to go see her family at least once a month, but in Neosho, 500 miles away from home, she was very lonely. She was a farm girl who had always lived close to her children and grandchildren and could see them whenever she wanted to. I had heard you can take a girl off a farm, but you can't take the farm out of the girl, and that proved true for us.

On one occasion, she went back to her home in Harvard, Nebraska, for a visit, and when I picked her up at the airport she called me mister. Not honey, but mister! I knew then that our marriage was in trouble, and I should have paid more attention to her needs. However, I was too busy playing golf and serving the church. The next time she went home, she called and said she wasn't coming back. She filed for divorce and sent her son-in-law to pick up her things. I was shocked about the abruptness of her decision, but not totally surprised that she had filed. We parted as friends and still stay in touch.

A member of the Neosho church introduced me to a "singles group" in Joplin, Missouri. I met a lady named Donna at that group, and we became good friends and dancing partners. She went with me to Lincoln when I officiated at the funeral of my mother. After the Neosho church called a minister, I spent some time traveling, and then settled down in Lincoln in an apartment across the street from my dad.

I had only been in Lincoln a few months when I was offered an interim at First Presbyterian in Parsons, Kansas, so I moved there early in 1990. When that interim ended in 1991, I retired at age 65 and moved back to Lincoln. Thus began another chapter in my life.

*Ardyce and Me,
circa 1988*

Chapter 27

RETIREMENT IN LINCOLN
1991 TO 1993

O nce again, I moved into an apartment across the street from my dad. We had breakfast together a couple times a week and spent time getting reacquainted. I'd call him or look in on him every day. Carolyn was glad to finally have a break from taking care of him and my mother after all those years. My days were spent playing pool, golfing, and seeing old friends. At night, I went dancing at a place called Sheri's or at the Pla Mor Ballroom. Occasionally, I would go watch the Cornhuskers play football.

One night, at the Pla Mor, I met Don and AnnaBelle Darnell. Don was a fraternity brother from Wesleyan. He told me he had written a book about dancing, and that I was in one of the chapters. What he wrote relates to the title of this book and I've included it in a later chapter.

Since dad had left me as executor of his estate, I spent most of 1992 taking care of that business. However, as you'll read in the next chapter, my life changed big time when I answered an ad in a magazine and moved to Omaha to become a cruise ship dance host.

Chapter 28

LIFE AS A DANCE HOST

After my dad died, I found retired life very boring. You can only play so much pool at the Senior Center, play golf only so many days a week, and go dancing so many nights a week. One day, I was reading a magazine called *Dancing USA*, when I come across an ad stating men who like to dance are needed to become Dance Hosts on cruise ships.

Arrangements were made for me to go to Chicago for an interview, where I was offered the job, and began my life as a Dance Host. The nice thing about it was they would offer you a cruise and you could decide whether you wanted to go or not. Most cruises were only for a couple weeks, with a few for a month or more. The cruise line paid your air transportation to and from the ports of embarkation and provided you with a shared cabin plus all meals.

My first cruise was on a riverboat, the *Mississippi Queen*, headed for New Orleans. After that, it was to Alaska, Hawaii, and every island in the Caribbean. I went through the Panama Canal twice and saw parts of the world I'd only heard about or seen pictures of in magazines.

My cruising culminated in 2001 with a round-the-world 97-day cruise with 35 ports of call. It began in Los Angeles and ended in New York. Highlights were Auckland, New Zealand; Sydney, Australia; Hong Kong; China; Singapore; Mumbai, India; Suez Canal and Port Said, Egypt; Haifa, Israel; Venice, Italy; Motril, Spain; and Lisbon, Portugal. We cruised the Strait of Gibraltar and headed back across the Atlantic to Fort Lauderdale, and then disembarked at New York. WHAT A TRIP! However, dancing six nights a week wore me out, and I was ready for some R and R!

My only cost for cruising was the $25 a day I paid my agent, furnishing my own clothing and dance shoes, and whatever I chose to spend on personal items and souvenirs when ashore. My only obligations were to dance with the ladies and escort any lady ashore who wanted company. I made lifetime friends, many of whom are still on my emails.

Over the years, I've had many men say, "Wow! That sounds like a fun job." My answer is, "You are right on both counts; it's fun and a job!" The fun is seeing the world on cruise ships and meeting interesting people with very little personal expense involved. The job is dancing at all hours of the day and night, even when you don't feel like it, smiling and being a gentleman even when some of the ladies treat you like a hired hand. Oh yes, sharing a room with a man you've never met isn't always that much fun either. Some smoke, some drink too much, and some violate the rules and are put off the ship and sent home at their own expense.

There were three rules while on duty: NO smoking; NO drinking to excess; NO hanky-panky! Of course, no rule said you couldn't get a phone number or two and make arrangements to meet a lady after the cruise was over. I think I might have done that a time or two!

When I wasn't cruising, I found many places to dance in Lincoln and Omaha. One night, while dancing at Peony Park in Omaha, I met Marilyn. She offered me a downstairs room in her home and we became dance partners during an off and on relationship for the next five years. She introduced me to Judy and Lou and Joyce Cavaleri. Lou became a best friend and got me started in officiating at weddings. Marilyn, Judy, and I became charter members of a dance club in Omaha. Marilyn moved to St. Louis to be with family. Judy is now married to Mick Merrick, and I see them when I'm out dancing. Stan, a member of the dance club, became a dance host, and we shared a cabin on a cruise; once was enough for him!

Life on a cruise ship around the world 2001

AROUND THE WORLD ON A CRUISE SHIP!

THE WORLD IS EXCITING TO SEE,
BUT HOME IS THE PLACE TO BE.

NINETY-SEVEN DAYS IS A LONG TIME TO BE AWAY,
EVEN IF YOU FIND PORTS WHERE YOU'D LIKE TO STAY.

MANY INTERESTING AND EXOTIC PLACES.
MANY PEOPLE OF VARYING BELIEFS AND RACES.

EAT FABULOUS FOOD WITH QUANTITIES GALORE,
END UP LOSING FIVE-TEN POUNDS OR MORE!

MUST HAVE BEEN THE COUNTLESS DANCING, DANCING,
RESTRICTIONS MADE SURE IT WASN'T THE ROMANCING.

NOW IT'S BACK TO REALITY IN NEBRASKA,
WONDERING IF I SHOULD GO BACK TO ALASKA.

STILL REMEMBER ALL THE NICE PEOPLE I MET,
TRYING TO TIE THEM TOGETHER IN MY E-MAIL NET.

SO KEEP IN TOUCH WHEN AND HOW YOU CAN,
UNTIL WE MEET AGAIN IN GOD'S MASTER PLAN.

Gil Hill (2001)

Dance Hosts Need Volunteer Attitude

THE WASHINGTON POST

In the movie "Out to Sea," Jack Lemmon and Walter Matthau are mismatched brothers-in-law who wind up as dance hosts seeking love — and wealth — aboard a cruise ship in the Caribbean.

In real life, said a recruiter who finds "gentleman hosts" for the cruise lines, the two probably never would have qualified to be dance hosts.

Lauretta Blake, owner of the Working Vacation, said that the movie has resulted in a mild increase in applications by men who want to trade their dance and social skills for a discounted cruise. However, the role of a gentleman host is no different, said Ms. Blake, "than helping out in a church organization, the Red Cross or the Peace Corps. You have to have a volunteer's attitude."

Ms. Blake places speakers, activity directors (fitness counselors, bridge instructors and the like) and entertainment assistants on the ships of seven cruise lines — Cunard, Delta Queen Steamboat Co., Holland America Line, Orient Lines, Regal Cruises and Silversea Cruises.

"Right now the speakers that we have a need for are people who do cultural things, who are able to talk about the destinations. Then we help with finding dance instructors, craft instructors, youth directors."

Those who pass a rigorous interview and background check may be matched with a ship. Successful applicants pay Ms. Blake's firm $25 for each day of the cruise and in return get a free cruise.

If doing the merengue is almost like walking to you, send an application to the Working Vacation, 610 Pine Grove Court, New Lenox, Ill. 60451. (No phone calls, please.)

Saturday, June 06, 2015

Articles about cruising

Gorgeous sunset—
you should see this one in color in my ebook!

" Song of a desperate dancing lady"

On this ship there are captains and even some kings,
There are men who are wearing great big diamond rings,
There are tenors,magicians and movie stars too,
There are authors and chef's and a very large crew,
There are sailors who've sailed every ocean and sea,
But whoever they are, they are nothing to me,
They could just as well be just a gaggle of ghosts,
For I only have eyes for the gentlemen hosts.

On the Rotterdam, the ones I want most,
are the men who are called Gentlemen hosts.
They're the ones I adore, all the others I ignore.
Some may look like Tom Hanks;   I tell'em "No Thanks",
Some may look like Tom Cruise;   their offers I refuse.
Some may be Sean Connery doubles;   to me they are mere bubbles.
Some may be football heroes;   to me they are all zeroes.
I disdain all their boasts   .I disdain all their toasts.
I only have eyes for the gentlemen hosts.

Alan, Victor,Bill and Simon You are def-i-nit-ely my men,
BW,Julian,Gil and Lou,I ab-so-lute-ly worship you,
Simon,Alan,Gil and Bill,of you I never get my fill.

Dear Gentlemen hosts, I adore you. Dear Gentlemen hosts, I implore you,,DONT ASK HER OR
HER OR HER, ASK ME, ASK ME, ASK ME,ASK ME.
I'M A DANCING LADY, PLEASE GIVE ME A CHANCE TO DANCE AND DANCE AND DANCE
AND DANCE.'

This is a song written by a lady on the world cruise about the dance hosts.

Chapter 29

LIFE WITH NANCY

As I said, prior to going on the world cruise in 2001, I met Nancy at a dance at the American Legion. She later told me she had seen me at Christian singles dances in Omaha, but I was too busy with the other ladies to notice her. One night, in the winter of 2000, a few of us from the Legion decided to go to a dance at the Starlite Ballroom in Wahoo, Nebraska. Five of us were coming home from the dance in a friend's car. I was sitting in the back seat between Nancy and another lady, Jackie, when I mentioned my dance shoes bag needed mending. Nancy spoke up and said she would be glad to do it. That led to a couple dates before I sailed away on the cruise. We communicated by email while I was gone. After the cruise, we continued dating until she grounded me.

Sometime later in 2001, my grandson, Shawn Hamilton, called and asked if I would officiate at his wedding to his girlfriend, Sunny. He gave me a date of March 30, 2002, and the Elvis Presley Chapel in Las Vegas as the place.

One day, Nancy and I were having breakfast when I said to her, "How about making the wedding in Las Vegas a double?"

After saying, "You aren't supposed to kid around about stuff like that!" she found out I was serious. She accepted my proposal, and we made plans to get married.

We chose The Little White Chapel on Las Vegas Boulevard because their weddings went over the web to anyone who wanted to watch them. We set our date for March 31, 2002, which just happened to be on Easter Sunday. Members of my family and their friends would already be in Vegas for Shawn's wedding, making it easy for them to attend. My sister went with us and served as matron of honor. My son-in-law, Gary Hamilton, was best man. George and Becky Esslinger, friends from Clovis, who lived in Vegas, furnished Nancy with a beautiful bridal bouquet. Alan Scott, a dance host friend, was in town, and came to the wedding. Unfortunately, Nancy's family couldn't be there, but two friends of hers who live in Las Vegas, Bill and Ardie Beeler, came for the wedding, and afterwards, we went out to eat and explored the city.

We returned to Omaha and moved into a third floor apartment at Benz Place. For Nancy, it was a move across town. For me, it was a move from a one-bedroom apartment at 305 Benz Place into a two-bedroom apartment overlooking the swimming pool at 308 Benz Place. Without an elevator, we have learned to go up and down the 27 stair steps with increasing care. I've fallen both going up and going down the stairs. I think the Lord is saying, "It's time to move to the first floor before you kill yourself." Someday soon I'll have to listen!

Because Nancy's family and our Omaha friends couldn't attend the wedding in Las Vegas we rented the Benz Place party room for a restatement of our vows. On June 14, 2002, Bob Thune, our pastor and friend from Christ Community Church officiated. Nancy's son Jim and family, her daughter Dawn and family and my son, Dennis and family were there, plus a few invited guests.

We continue to dance on Friday nights at the Legion, and she gives me permission to dance once or twice a week with all my friends at the Ozone, a dance venue in Omaha. Many friends, both male and female, remark that they hope they can move like me when they are my age. I just say, "Thank you! I'd rather wear out than rust out!"

OUR BLENDED FAMILIES

I could write another book about our blended families, but will keep to the basics for this one.

I have three children, eight grandchildren, and nine great-grandchildren. Nancy has three children, eight grandchildren, and one great.

My daughter, Pam, is married to Gary, and they have two sons, Shawn and Seth, and a daughter, Shannon. Shawn is married to Sunny, and they have two daughters, Savannah and Samantha. Seth is married to Holly, and they have one son, Colton, and three daughters, Hartley, Stella, and Everly. Shannon has one son, Connor. Pam and Gary are raising Connor.

My son, David, is married to Jeannie, and they have one son, Clinton, who is married to Tracey. Clinton and Tracey have two children, a son, Jackson, and a daughter, Harper.

My son, Dennis, is married to Mary, and they have two sons, Kent and Jack, and two daughters, Abbey and Madeline. Kent is married to Amy.

I've had the privilege of officiating at the weddings for all three of my children and for three of my grandchildren.

Nancy's daughter, Dawn, has two daughters, Melanie and Meredith.

Nancy's daughter, Pat, has two married sons, Taylor, who is married to Mercedes, and Murphy, who is married to Kalah. Pat's son, Cooper, a twin to Murphy, and Pat's daughter, Dakota, are both single.

Nancy's son, Jim, has two sons, Jackson and Grant.

My dad, when asked how many grandchildren he had, would always say, "Seven that I know of!" So these are the families we know of! By the time this book goes to press, there will probably be additions we know of!

Our families reside in Florida, New Mexico, Texas, California, Iowa, and Nebraska, which gives us nice places to visit, but makes it almost impossible to have a family gathering. In fact, we are yet to have them all in the same place at the same time. Maybe for my funeral!

Up next, life in Omaha!

Nancy - 4 siblings and spouses - 1990

Ruthie Nancy Gil Pastor
6-14-02   Bob

At our second wedding in Omaha

Nancy and Me on our
wedding day in Vegas
March 31, 2002

Chapter 30

LIFE IN OMAHA

It is hard to believe, but living over 20 years in Omaha is longer than the time spent in any other town. My vagabond life style has included over 30 moves and included these places: Chadron, Nebraska; Lincoln, Nebraska; Table Rock, Nebraska; Blair, Nebraska; Pueblo, Colorado; St. Paul, Minnesota; Broomfield, Colorado; Kansas City, Missouri; Clovis, New Mexico; Fairfield, Nebraska; Kearney, Nebraska; Fremont, Nebraska; Neosho, Missouri; Parsons, Kansas; and Omaha.

Since writing about life in Omaha needs more than one chapter, I've decided to use sub-headings, beginning with that which God called me to do—Ministry.

I've served two Presbyterian churches as pulpit supply, Castelar in Omaha and

Gethsemane in Council Bluffs, Iowa, each for about a year. I'm presently preaching twice a month at New Cassel Retirement Home, a place where Nancy used to work.

At the church we attend, Christ Community, in Omaha, I've had opportunities to teach Bible classes, officiate at weddings, baptize Nancy and other friends, and pray for people who come forward for healing. Nancy sings in the choir with some of her friends from Sweet Adelines. It's a Christian Missionary Alliance Church, and we are blessed to worship there and be a part of their mission to the world.

However, my main ministry in and around Omaha has been officiating at weddings. Lou Cavaleri, who I mentioned previously, had a business called The Omaha Bridal Show. Soon after we met, he offered me a booth at his shows where I could talk to brides about officiating at their upcoming weddings. That opportunity launched me into a ministry to where I've now helped over 300 couples tie the knot.

A book about the people I've met and the weddings I've done would make a best seller, but I'll just leave that to your imagination. The fact that I keep getting referrals and have married children of couples I'd married is an indication that I've been doing something right. It's discouraging to know that fifty percent of the couples getting married don't make it, but I keep praying for all of them.

Log on to my web site GILHILL.NET if you'd like to see me in action. The couple being married is my grandson, Seth Hamilton, to Holly, and it took place on St. Thomas Island in the Caribbean on March 22, 2004.

OMAHA BIRTHDAYS

I've celebrated so many birthdays in Omaha I've lost track of them, but a few are worth mentioning in this book. So many have been at the Ozone, where I dance, that friends are saying, "Another birthday, Gil?" To which I answer, "Sure beats the alternative!"

One memorable birthday was my 80th in 2006, when I celebrated it on two different days. The first was on April 23 at American Legion Post 1 where over 100 family and friends signed the guest book. Out of town guests included former members of Westminster P.C. in Clovis, New Mexico. They were Gary and Jan Britt, Gary and Sheila Engel, Richard and Eileen Koskie, and Ron and Janet Syrcle.

The second 80th birthday celebration was held in the clubhouse at Benz Place, primarily for our families, but with a few friends who couldn't come to the first party. My daughter and family and my two sons and their families were there along with Nancy's son and family and one of her two daughters and family. My sister and her family were also there. It was the closest we've ever come to having our blended families all in one place. Lord willing, I'll have a 90th birthday in 2016!

I have an album about my 83rd birthday on April 22, 2009, when I was on an "Honor Flight" to Washington, D.C. to see the World War II Memorial. On that flight I had one of those "divine appointments." We were on a chartered 747 with 375 veterans and 25 volunteers on board. During part of the flight I was seated next to Bill Williams, who, with his wife Yvonne, organized all of the honor flights for war veterans. They have also done a fantastic job of creating "Remember the Fallen," a display of pictures and memories of those who were killed during our wars. They have become good friends and Bill has asked me to give the invocation at some of the honor flights and reunions.

On the night of my 83rd, Nancy and I attended a pre-flight dinner at the Holiday Inn in Omaha.

We spent the night there and I arose to catch a 5:00 a.m. bus to the airport. In groping around in the dark, I forgot my keys were in my carry-on and I picked up Nancy's keys and took them with me. OOPS! Senior Moment! I later learned she had a friend take her bowling and was able to go with the other wives on a planned tour of the Durham Museum. Realizing I might get back at midnight and head for the car, she left a note on the car windshield which read, "You have my keys!" All's well that ends well, and we both got home safely in the wee hours of the morning.

While on the trip I made friends with another Navy veteran, Wes S., from Lincoln, who had also been a high school athletic coach and teacher. We spent most of the day in Washington together and had our picture taken with congressmen and senators from Nebraska who were there to greet us. Highlights for the day included The Tomb of the Unknown Soldier, Arlington Cemetery, and the Iwo Jima Memorial.

The flight to Washington and back and seeing all the sites took place on one day, from 5:00 a.m. to midnight. Many veterans had canes and walkers and some were in wheelchairs. Since I was exhausted, it's hard to imagine how tired they must have been.

As I always say, "Act young as long as you can, there will be time enough to be old!"

CHRIST COMMUNITY CHURCH

As I mentioned before, Nancy and I attend Christ Community Church when we aren't traveling or I'm not preaching somewhere.

In the fall of 2013, I was teaching the Ambassadors Class for seniors. One Sunday when they were honoring veterans, we were asked to bring a picture of the time when we were in the service. I brought my picture of when I was in the Navy, and happened to show it to a member of the class, Bill Arnold. What happened next is in this article from *Horizon*, a local monthly newspaper.

NAVY VETS MEET 69 YEARS AFTER BASIC TRAINING

In June 1944, a couple of Nebraska teenagers, Gil Hill from Chadron, and Bill Arnold of Omaha, arrived at the Farragut Naval Station in Idaho to begin nine weeks of basic training during World War II. Although both were assigned to Camp Hill and Company 669, Arnold and Hill never met one another during their Idaho days despite sharing the same barracks.

After basics, Hill, then 18, was sent to the South Pacific where he served for two years on an AK-230 ship named the *USS Manderson Victory*. "We had 8,000 tons of ammo aboard," Hill said during a recent interview. "Our job was to supply ammo for the battleships, cruisers, and destroyers."

Following basic training and a stint at a naval fleet post office in San Francisco, Arnold, then age 18, was shipped to Guam where he served for 10 months. Discharged from the Navy in 1946, Arnold spent 38 years at United of Omaha, retiring from the insurance company in 1988 as vice-president in the firm's investment division.

Hill, also discharged in 1946, retired in 1992 after careers as a high school coach and a Presbyterian minister.

Flash forward to July 2013 when Hill was a guest teacher of a Bible study class at Omaha's Christ Community Church. He learned that a congregation member was putting together a book that would feature current and past photos of CCC members who had served in the United States Military.

Arnold, who was taking the Bible class, and Hill began comparing notes about their days in the Navy. The pair was amazed to discover they were finally meeting 69 years after being stationed at the same base, assigned to the same company, and living in the same barracks.

"Meeting Hill and learning we had so much in common was quite a surprise," a smiling Arnold said during a recent interview.

"I was astonished," Hill said. "I thought it had to be an act of God."

These days, Arnold, who had two children with his first wife, Marilyn, enjoys spending time with Evelyn, his spouse since 2003. Despite injuring his shoulder in a fall last winter, the 87-year-old grandfather of three plans to take up golfing again as soon as he heals.

Hill, who has three children, eight grandchildren, and nine great grandchildren, has been married to his third wife, Nancy, since 2002. Gil, at age 89, golfs twice a week, and keeps busy providing counseling and helping out with weddings and funerals.

Hill and Arnold have become good friends, have lunch together from time to time, and still can't believe they met 69 years after being in the Navy in the same time and in the same location.

"What are the odds of that happening," said Hill. "Probably like the odds of winning the lottery."

Navy vets meet 69 years after basic training

Gil Hill today and as a 18-year-old member of the United States Navy.

In June 1944, a couple of Nebraska teenagers, Gil Hill from Chadron and Bill Arnold of Omaha, arrived at the Farragut Naval Station in Idaho to begin nine weeks of basic training during World War II. Although both were assigned to Camp Hill and Company 669, Arnold and Hill never met one another during their Idaho days despite sharing the same barracks.

After basics, Hill, then age 18, was sent to the South Pacific where he served for two years on an AK-230 ship named the USS Manderson Victory.

"We had 8,000 tons of ammo aboard," Hill said during a recent interview. "Our job was to supply ammo for the battleships, cruisers, and destroyers."

Following basic training and a stint at a naval fleet post office in San Francisco, Arnold, then age 18, was shipped to Guam where he served for 10 months.

Discharged from the Navy in 1946, Arnold spent 38 years at United of Omaha, retiring from the insurance company in 1988 as a vice-president in the firm's investment division.

Hill, also discharged in 1946, retired in 1992 after careers as a high school coach and a Presbyterian minister.

Flash forward to July 2013 when Hill was a guest teacher of a Bible study class at Omaha's Christ Community Church. He learned that a congregation member was putting together a book that would feature current and past photos of CCC members who had served in the United States military.

Arnold who was taking that Bible class and Hill began comparing notes about their days in the Navy. The pair was amazed to discover they were finally meeting 69 years after being stationed at the same base, assigned to the same company, and living in the same barracks.

"It (meeting Hill and learning the men had so much in common) was quite a surprise," a smiling Arnold said during a recent interview.

"I was astonished," Hill said. "I thought it had to be an act of God."

These days, Arnold – who had two children with his first wife, Marilyn – enjoys spending time with Evelyn, his spouse since 2003. Despite injuring his shoulder in a fall last winter, the 87-year-old grandfather of three, plans to take up golfing again as soon as he heals.

Hill, who has three children, eight grandchildren, and eight great-grandchildren, has been married to his second wife, Nancy, for 11 years. His first wife, Melva, died of cancer in 1985. The Hills had been married for 35 years.

Gil, also age 87, golfs twice a week, and keeps busy providing counseling and helping out with weddings and funerals.

Hill and Arnold have become good friends, have lunch together from time to time, and still can't believe they met 69 years after being in basic training at the same time and in the same location.

"What are the odds of that happening," said Hill. "Probably like the odds of winning the lottery."

6th HEARTLAND HONOR FLIGHT

Pre-Flight Dinner
Wednesday, April 22, 2009
Holiday Inn Central, Omaha

Welcome
Bill & Evonne Williams

Bob Scudder, Emcee

Marine Corps Honor Guard
Engineer Maintenance Company, Omaha

Star Spangled Banner
Janet Campbell, Mezzo-soprano
Lois Carlsen, Piano

Willowdale Swing Choir
Willowdale Elementary, Millard Public Schools
Barbara Carlsen, Director

Invocation
Pastor Carlos Schneider
Kountze Memorial Lutheran Church, Omaha

Dinner

Governor Dave Heineman

Larry Cappetto
Filmmaker and producer of the television
documentary "Lest They Be Forgotten"

America the Beautiful
Janet Campbell and Lois Carlsen

Armed Forces Medley
Lois Carlsen, Piano

Let There Be Peace On Earth
Micki Marr, Alto

Benediction
Pastor Carlos Schneider

Retirement of the Colors

THANKS TO VETTER HEALTH SERVICES
FOR SPONSORING TONIGHT'S EVENT

Before we left for the honor flight

In D.C. in front of the Iwo Jima Memorial

Me and Wes Shepard

80th Birthday - American Legion Post 1

Blended family gathered for my 80th Birthday, 2006

Former Westminster Church members came to my 80th
birthday, 2006. From Missouri, Oklahoma, and Texas.

My son Dennis Hill at my 85th birthday

Chapter 31

PLAYING GOLF

I started playing golf in 1949, when I was a senior in college at Nebraska Wesleyan University. I qualified for their first ever golf team and earned a letter. I continued playing while a Caddy Master at Lincoln Country Club in the summer of 1950. After Melva and I got married and began having children, I put the clubs away. When we moved to Pueblo, a friend asked me to join the Country Club and play golf with him. I established a handicap and soon was playing to a 12.

While working in Rapid City, South Dakota, I entered a handicap tournament with a friend and we won first place. I kept my clubs in the trunk of my car and hit the links whenever I had spare time during my travels around that state.

I didn't have time to play while in seminary, but after graduation I played a number of times with James Jeffrey in and around Kansas City.

After moving to Clovis, I started playing on Mondays, my day off, with some other pastors. I put together a pastor's golf tournament on May 24, 1976, and was rewarded with my first hole-in-one on a par 3, 149-yard hole, at the Municipal Golf Course.

I played many different courses during the time I was serving churches in other places. After I retired, I was blessed with my second hole-in-one on July 29, 1994, on a par 3, 179-yard hole, over a lake at Pioneer Golf Course in Lincoln, Nebraska. I have certificates hanging on my office wall attesting to both holes-in-one! Still looking for number three!

While living in Lincoln, Syd Carne called and invited me to join his golf group, The Dirty Dozen, out of Omaha. I'd met Syd while in Kansas City, and we'd kept in touch over the years. He's now playing golf in Heavenly places!

After I moved to Omaha, I joined Easter Nebraska Seniors and at one of their events, I was paired with Frank Hartle. He became my partner for some other events and before long my best friend. When Syd couldn't play any longer due to health problems, he asked me to take over The Dirty Dozen. I, in turn, asked Frank to help. I'm the chief tee-time getter, and Frank's the handicapper.

We've been coordinating this golf group for over 15 years. In that time ten members have died and new members have joined. We subsequently changed the name to The Good Ole Boys since we have more than 12 players. Now we have anywhere from 12 to 16 golfers playing twice a week, Monday and Wednesday, in season. In season in Nebraska is whenever it doesn't snow, rain, or the wind blows you off the tee box. We usually conclude our season with an annual tourney. We manage to play 20-30 different courses every year, all within a 50 mile radius of Omaha.

If you've ever tried to lead a group of any kind, I'm sure you learned the axiom, "You can please some of the people some of the time, most of the people most of the time, but you can't please all the people all of the time." I found that true in athletics, as a coach, and as a minister. It's definitely true when trying to lead a group of senior golfers. There will always be someone who thinks they could do a better job at whatever you are doing. Many times I've gotten frustrated enough to resign from the scheduling of golf courses, but I'm still hanging in there. I've decided that, after I die,

I'll have my ashes scattered on some of the golf courses we've played so I can trip somebody up and get even!

An avid golfer asked his pastor if there are any golf courses in Heaven. His pastor checked it out and came back saying, "I've good news and bad news for you! The good news is that the best golf courses in the universe are in Heaven, but the bad news is you have a tee time tomorrow morning at 9:00 a.m."

I have at least forty or fifty more golf jokes if you'd like to hear them!

Fox Run, Council Bluffs, 2006
Jim (Nancy's son), David (my son), Me

Chapter 32

BACK TO RUNNING TRACK

I had competed in track while in high school and college, so while living in Neosho, Missouri, and finding myself single again, I decided to go back to the track. One day, I read in the Joplin newspaper that they were holding senior games in track, so I decided to enter. Because dancing and golf had kept me in good physical shape, I was able to win a number of medals, with a gold medal coming in race-walking.

After I retired and moved to Lincoln, I was told about the Cornhusker Games, held annually, where you competed with your own age group in five-year segments. At my suggestion they put in race-walking, and, once again, I was able to win a gold medal in my age group. At that time I was in the 60-65 group.

When I learned they also had State Games in track, held annually in Kearney, Nebraska, I began competing in track events there; first in race-walking and then in the 100, 200, and 400 meters. I continued to do that when I wasn't on a cruise ship, winning medals which now are in a drawer in my closet, gathering dust.

That culminated when, at age 78, I had a five gold medal day, and it was written up in the *New Horizon* newspaper. (Published here by permission)

Back to the Track

After three years away from the track to let my body and feet heal, I returned to the track in 2015. On one of my trips to the VA for a medical check-up, I saw a pamphlet advertising the VA Senior Golden Age Games, which were to be held in Omaha that year. So I signed up for the 100- and 200-yard dashes and the one mile power walk. The track events took place on Sunday morning, August 9 at Burke High School. I placed first in all three events in my age group, 85 to 89. As I completed the 100-yard dash, a young lady approached me and asked if she and a camera man could interview me for television.

Of course, I said okay. She asked me to state my name, age, where I was from, and anything else I'd like to add. I closed the interview with my standard remark, "I still compete because I'd rather wear out than rust out." That same evening my 30 seconds of fame was on Channel 9 in Omaha during both the 6pm and 10pm news!

Subsequently, a number of people told me they saw the interview.

Take care of your body, my friends; you only get one trip around!

Retired minister wins five gold medals at Senior Games!

By George Reinhardt
Contributing Writer

Gil Hill, a 78-year-old retired Presbyterian minister, loves competing in sports. That's why he has been so active in the Nebraska Senior Games for the past 12 years.

> "That's my goal now; to live to be 100 and still compete."

During this year's August games in Kearney, Hill won five gold medals in golf and track. He fired an 84 to win the golf medal, the best round he has had in recent years. He also won gold medals in the 1,500-meter race walk, the 100-meter dash, the 200-meter dash, and the 400-meter dash. He bettered his times in each event over last year, which surprised him since he hadn't been able to work out as much recently

because of a sore hip.

Hill has won so many gold medals in the state games; he's lost track of the total. He's given so many of the gold medals to his grandkids they now tell him, "Grandpa, we don't want any more."

Hill has always loved competing in sports.

Gil Hill with his five gold medals!

When he was in high school at Chadron, Neb. he won two letters each in football, basketball, and track. In college, he earned four letters in football and track at Nebraska Wesleyan. After college, he was a high school coach at Table Rock and Blair, Neb. and Pueblo, Colo.

While coaching at Pueblo Gil said he "met the Lord for the first time, and four years later he called me to the ministry."

At age 35, with a wife and three little children, Hill entered the ministry in Kansas City, Mo. He served God as a minister for 30 years at different churches around the country.

When he retired from the ministry in 1992, Hill returned to Nebraska, and competed in the Nebraska Senior Games for the first time.

Hill stays in shape by playing golf three times a week, racquetball three times a week, and prepares for the track events by regularly walking the golf course. While his golfing partners ride the cart from shot to shot, Gil does it all on foot. During the winter months, he continues his workouts at the Downtown YMCA.

Hill loves competing in sports so much that he plans to do so "til I die. I'd rather wear out than rust out."

He remembers a 93-year-old lady he met during his first state games.

"She said something I will never forget. 'I've learned how to win. I've outlived them all.' So that's my goal now; to live to be 100 and still compete."

Sr. Olympics - Kearney, Nebraska
"Two Winners"
Dick Weaver and Gil Hill August 20, 2000

ACKNOWLEDGMENTS

Writing this book has been a labor of love and learning. I learned you can't write an autobiography without using a lot of personal pronouns. I also learned that my memory, although still good, isn't as sharp as it used to be. I'm like the man that said, "I've seen it all, heard it all, and done it all. I just can't remember it all!"

I'm indebted to Mona Pomeroy of Clovis, New Mexico for reading every page, offering suggestions, and correcting my punctuation.

Thanks to Lisa Pelto, President of Concierge Marketing, and her staff, Ellie, Rachel and Sarah, for their help in publishing.

Since this book is about *The Dancing Preacher* I've decided to include the words from another book in which I'm referred to as both a preacher and a dancer. Don Darnell, a college classmate and fraternity brother, began dancing late in life with his wife, AnnaBelle. After he retired from being a high school teacher and principal, he wrote a book about "the heroic exploits in the intimate dance lives of an 'old' couple swinging through their sixties." Here is an excerpt about me from Don's book, printed with his permission.

Talents, and there are many different kinds, are God given. But, one of the realities of life is that they are not equally distributed. Some people seem to have more natural ability than others. The Dancin' Preacher is one of those individuals.

The first time I remember seeing him, he was neither dancing nor preaching. In the late 1940s, we were both students at Nebraska Wesleyan University. I sat next to him in an English Literature class. He may also have been taking education courses in preparation to teach at the secondary school level. But, of all those who knew him as a very amiable, outgoing person, only a few would have wagered that he would become "a man of the cloth."

In the early 1980s I saw him again in a small town about sixty miles from Lincoln. Another principal and I were attending the funeral of the father of Lincoln High School's football coach. We arrived in the town early, found the church, went in, and sat down. The minister was busy making preparations for the service. As we sat there, I mentioned to the other principal—also a Wesleyan graduate—that from a profile view, the clergyman looked like our old college friend. He responded with something like, "Darnell, you have to be kidding. There is no way that he would be a preacher." Well it turned out he was our college friend, in the flesh, and, indeed, he was the preacher.

Without notes, and only referring several times to certain Biblical passages, he delivered one of the most eloquent, personal eulogies that I have ever heard. And it was for someone he didn't even know. After the service, we had the opportunity to visit with him briefly and renew our friendship.

A few years later, AnnaBelle and I were at the Pla Mor Ballroom for a Wednesday Night Singles Dance. Early in the evening, we saw a couple in the center of the floor who were dancing the jitterbug. They were the talk and the focus of attention. It had been a long, long time since I had seen dancers doing the jitterbug steps like they were originally intended. They were dancing the way I remember the sailors danced in the USO's during World War II.

When we circled the dance floor, we got close enough to identify him. Again, I couldn't believe who I saw: It was my old college friend, the preacher in the flesh. Now he was the Dancin' Preacher.

Renewing our friendship that evening was both joyful and depressing. Joyful to see him again, but depressing on finding out that his wife had recently died. I was reminded again that even God's ministers, like all of us, are not immune to life's personal tragedies. My good friend, the preacher, had learned, in order to heal a broken heart and retain a positive, spiritual attitude toward life, both figuratively and literally, YOU GOTTA KEEP DANCING!

MORE CREDITS...

It would be impossible for me to give personal credit to everyone who has touched my life in meaningful ways through the years, so I will just list the groups. If you are in one of those groups, please know I am grateful for your touch. It has been said, "Some people come into your life for a reason, some for a season, and some to take up residence in your heart."

Those who touched my life for a reason are:

1. My parents and their extended families.

2. My teachers in grade school, high school, college, and seminary.

3. The young ladies who first taught me how to dance.

4. My classmates at Chadron High School.

5. My classmates and fraternity brothers at Nebraska Wesleyan.

6. Those I met while I was a high school teacher and coach.

7. The men who first introduced me to Jesus Christ.

8. My classmates at Midwestern Baptist Seminary.

9. All those who ever called me Pastor!

Those who have touched my life for a season are:

1. Those I met while in the Navy.

2. Those who were in one of the eight churches I served as a minister.

3. Those I had the privilege of baptizing.

4. Those I met when I officiated at their wedding.

5. Those I've met on the dance floor.

6. Those I've met on the golf course.

7. Those I've met at Christ Community Church.

8. Those I've met at New Cassel Retirement Home.

9. All those who ever called me friend!

Those who have taken up residence in my heart are:

1. Ward and Dora Hill, my parents.

2. Carolyn, my sister, and her family.

3. My three wives: Melva, Ardyce, and Nancy.

4. My three children: Pam, David, Dennis and their spouses. Gary married to Pam, Jeannie married to David, and Mary married to Dennis.

5. My eight grandchildren: Shawn, Seth, Shannon, Clinton, Kent, Abbey, Madeline, and Jack. Spouses, Sunny married to Shawn,

Holly married to Seth, Tracey married to Clinton, and Amy married to Kent.

6. My great-grandchildren; presently there are nine (more to be added).

7. Nancy's three children: Pat, Dawn, Jim and their children.

8. My Lord and Savior, Jesus Christ.

CONCLUSION
MY BUCKET LIST AND FINAL WORDS

I've seen the movie *The Bucket List* with Jack Nicholson and Morgan Freeman at least three times. It's about what they want to do before they die (i.e. kick the bucket). I found it fun to watch them as they went about doing the things on their bucket lists.

The movie prompted me to comprise my own bucket list. I've modified my list to five things I would like to do before I die and two I want to do after I die. Here's my list:

1. To stay healthy in mind, body, and spirit.
2. To attend the Master's Golf Tournament.
3. To attend the Kentucky Derby.
4. To publish my memoirs. (*Done!*)
5. To live to be 100.
6. To give the eulogy at my own funeral.
7. To go to Heaven.

I may not live to be 100 or attend the Masters or the Derby, but this book is number four on the list, and I've already put number six on tape with the help of my friend, Lee Taylor. I have the assurance that number seven will come to pass because Jesus said, "I go to prepare a place for you, and if I go to prepare a place for you, I will come again and take you unto myself, that where I am you will be also." (John 14:2-3)

Here, then, are my final words which those who come to my graduation ceremony to Heaven will hear. The other reason I put them on tape was so I wouldn't disappoint my son, David, who said, "You always had to have the last word!"

Greetings from Heaven. I'm here with Jesus, my mom and dad, sweet Melva, and all the saints who have gone before me. We are gathered around the throne and singing praises to the "Lamb of God, who takes away the sins of the world," and, every now and then, to stay in character, I get up and dance with the ladies.

Thanks for coming to my Victory Celebration! You came in to the big band music I've danced to over the years, and you've just heard the number one song on my spiritual hit parade, "Victory in Jesus."

When you leave, please humor me by marching out to the song, "When the Saints Come Marching In," and I'll see you later in the Promised Land.

I doubt if there is anyone here from high school days in Chadron, from college at Nebraska Wesleyan, or from the towns where I was a high school athletic coach and teacher, but, just in case, thank you for coming.

If you are here because we met on the dance floor, thanks for sharing your dances with the Dancing Preacher. If I stepped on your toes, I'm sorry, and if I was ever less than a gentleman, please forgive me. If you are one of the guys that said you'd like to be like me on the dance floor, it's all yours, so go for it!

If you are here because we had the opportunity to play golf together, my advice is be careful where you step next time you play; my ashes just might be underfoot.

If you are here because we met at church, then keep the faith, love Jesus and love people until Jesus returns or you join me in Heaven. If you are here because I had the privilege of being your pastor, then I need to remind you of what a blessing it was to serve you in that capacity. You are truly "the salt of the earth!"

If you are here because we are kinfolk, thank you for our time together on planet earth. Be assured you are in my heart and I'll be waiting for you in Heaven. I love each of you more than you can ever know or feel.

Nancy, thank you for being my soulmate and my wife. As my children could have told you, and you soon found out, I'm not an easy guy to live with. Thanks for staying the course and giving me a second family to love and enjoy. Keep on singing until we meet again. I agape you.

Pam and Gary, yours was a marriage made in Heaven, but lived out with all the ups and downs on earth. Thanks for the grandchildren and great-grandchildren you blessed me with. Pam, you have the sweet disposition of your mother and my smile. As Gary has said, "Pam, you look more like your dad every day," so, every time you look in the mirror, you will see my reflection looking back at you. Gary, you are and always will be my only son-in-law. We have been good for each other. I love each of you in the growing Hamilton family with an everlasting love.

David and Jeannie, you met in New Mexico, but lived out your lives in Texas. Thanks for keeping the Hill name going through Clinton. David, you have the tender nature of your mother and my athletic interests. Remember me the next time you hit a golf ball or go fishing. And Jeannie, thanks for teaching my grandson a foreign language. ("Y'all," "I'm fixing to," etc.) I love you and your extended family.

Dennis and Mary, you met in Hastings, Nebraska, were married in Omaha, Nebraska, and are living in Lincoln, Nebraska. Thanks to both of you for the beautiful family you gave me and the world. I wish we could have spent more time together on earth, but we'll have an eternity together to catch up. I love you and each and every member of your growing family.

Finally, let me encourage all of you concerning Heaven. As the song says, "When we all get to Heaven, what a day of rejoicing that will be!" If you haven't already, you'll want to get on the gospel train and join me in Heaven. Your ticket is the blood of Jesus, shed on Calvary for you and for me. Believe the Good News, accept Jesus as your Savior, and I'll meet you at the pearly gates. Amen and Amen.

19 To God Be the Glory

Fanny J. Crosby, 1820-1915

W. H. Doane, 1832-1915

1. To God be the glory—great things He hath done. So loved He the world that He
2. O perfect re-demp-tion, the purchase of blood, To ev-'ry be-liev-er the
3. Great things He hath taught us, great things He hath done, And great our rejoicing thro'

gave us His Son, Who yielded His life an a-tone-ment for sin, And opened the
prom-ise of God! The vil-est of-fend-er who tru-ly believes, That moment from
Je-sus, the Son; But pu-rer, and higher, and greater will be Our won-der, our

REFRAIN

Life-gate that all may go in.
Je-sus a par-don receives. Praise the Lord, praise the Lord, Let the earth hear His
transport, when Je-sus we see.

voice! Praise the Lord, praise the Lord, Let the peo-ple re-joice! O come to the

Fa-ther, thro' Je-sus, the Son, And give Him the glo-ry—great things He hath done.